Teenagers

face to face with

Bereavement

KAREN GRAVELLE

CHARLES HASKINS

AN AUTHORS GUILD BACKINPRINT.COM EDITION

AN AUTHORS GUILD BACKINPRINT.COM EDITION

Published by iUniverse.com, Inc.

For information address:
iUniverse.com, Inc.
5220 S 16th, Ste. 200
Lincoln, NE 68512
www.iuniverse.com

Originally published by Julian Mesner

OTHER BOOKS BY KAREN GRAVELLEN
Teenagers Face to Face with Cancer
(with Bertram A. John)

Animal Talk
(with Ann Squire)

ISBN: 0-595-15278-3

Printed in the United States of America

Contents

Contents

Introduction

OF THE seventeen young people who helped to write this book, all but one lost a parent, sibling, or close friend during adolescence. The exception is Colin, who was ten when his younger brother died. It's only recently, though, that Colin has had a chance to express some of his feelings about this loss. Now thirteen and part of a bereavement group for adolescents, he finds that his struggle to deal with grief is similar to the experience of other adolescents.

For some of these teenagers, the death was sudden and unexpected—four lost a brother or friend in an accident, while another two had fathers who died of heart attacks. For most, though, the death was a result of illness—cancer, cystic fibrosis, or the complications of alcoholism. Regardless of how death occurred or whether or not there was time to prepare, the pain was the same. As Abby says, "There's no good way to experience it."

These young people are at various stages in coming to terms with their loss. Some are now far enough away from the death that they can offer a perspective on the whole process. A few are recently bereaved, having lost someone within the past year. Most, however, are somewhere in the middle—over the initial shock and now trying to deal with the pain, anger, and guilt that follow.

Talking about their feelings with people who want to listen has been very important for them, whether it's been with parents, friends, or as in one case, pets. Because of this and because they hope it will help others, these young people want to tell you what losing someone they loved has been like for them. Their names are fictitious—but they and their experiences are very real.

NAME	AGE WHEN BEREAVED	PRESENT AGE	PERSON WHO DIED	CAUSE OF DEATH
			Parent	
Marie[1]	17	18	Father	Cancer
Lynette[1]	14	15	Father	Cancer
Vicky	12	16	Mother	Cancer
Megan	14	16	Mother	Cancer
Terry[2]	13	15	Mother	Cancer
Stephanie[2]	11	13	Mother	Cancer
Gary	14	16	Father	Heart attack
Kristen	14	15	Father	Heart attack
Erica	18	19	Stepmother	Complications of alcoholism
			Sibling	
Adam	15	18	Older Brother	Car accident
Abby	17	22	Older Brother	Car accident
Brenda	15	25	Older Brother	Hit by car
Jay	12	14	Older Sister	Cancer
Julie	12	15	Younger Brother	Cancer
Colin	10	13	Younger Brother	Cystic fibrosis
			Friend	
Elaine	12	23	Best Friend	Cancer
Pam	17	18	Boyfriend	Motorcycle accident

---
[1] Sisters
[2] Sisters

Part One
What Makes Adolescent Grief Different

GRIEF IS OUR response to the loss of a person we've loved. It can result from any separation that takes the loved one from us, including abandonment, divorce, and, of course, death. But because death is final and irreversible, because it permanently removes any hope of a further reunion, the grief that follows this loss is usually most intense.

Grieving involves both emotional and behavioral responses. Shock, denial, depression, anger, and isolation are only some of the reactions grieving people experience. In one way or another, people who have suffered the death of someone they loved must struggle to cope with these painful and confusing emotions, learn to accept their loss, and rebuild their lives.

Bereaved people of all ages pass through a series of stages in coming to grips with the death of someone close to them. Who the grieving person is at the start of this process, however, influences what these stages will be like. People of different ages obviously bring different experiences, needs, and concerns with them when they begin to confront their loss.

It has been said that grieving is a full time job. The same is certainly true of being an adolescent. Teenagers generally have their hands full just trying to separate from their families and establish their own identities and places in the world. To accomplish this, they need to feel that life is basically safe and that their parents will be there if needed.

For adolescents, therefore, the death of a family member or a close friend is more than just a horrible loss and cause of great pain. By ripping away their sense of security, the death makes it more difficult for them to do what other adolescents around them are doing—breaking away from their families and beginning to become independent adults.

Because of this, adolescent bereavement is different from that experienced by either younger children or adults, and bereaved teenagers face special problems in dealing with their loss.

1 / Stages of Adolescent Grief

It's usually about a year before you can talk about it. Because before you can tell people about it, you have to accept it. And it takes a while for that.—JULIE

It seems to me that it's getting worse before it gets better. That's not a good feeling—I wish I'd gotten it out of the way already.—ERICA

No one's grief follows a predetermined course. Not all bereaved people experience the same emotions in the same order or at the same time. But people who are grieving share many similar experiences and the process for most of them seems to take a common shape.

At first, most adults respond to the terrible news that someone they care about has died by becoming numb. This initial phase can last from a few hours to a week. In general, the bereaved person feels very little during this period. Every now and then, however, the numbness is pierced by intense emotions of extreme distress, anger, or both.

As this initial phase lifts, the grieving person enters a period of yearning and searching for the lost figure that continues for months or, sometimes, years. Overlapping with this yearning phase is a stage of disorganization and despair. Finally, with the acceptance of the death, the bereaved person reaches the last phase of mourning—a stage of reorganization.

While similar to adult mourning, the process of adolescent grieving is different in some respects. For one thing, it appears to take most teenagers longer to truly begin to mourn. While adults generally experience the first year as the time of most intense pain, adolescents are frequently numb for at least part of this period. Eight months to a year later, when they are flooded with overwhelming and conflicting emotions, it can come as a surprise to everyone.

Erica's stepmother, Sharon, died six months ago. Erica says, "Now I'm thinking about her more. And I want to deal with it more now." It's taken a while for it to register that Sharon is actually dead. "I still kept thinking she was going to come back. Or she would just show up some day," she adds. "And now, I realize she's not going to."

To her distress, Erica is finding that with time she's feeling worse, not better, about her loss. As the unreality of Sharon's death fades, Erica is having to face some painful and conflicting emotions. And she doesn't like this unexpected development at all.

Marie's experience has been somewhat different. In the period immediately following her father's death, she was obsessed with thoughts of him. "The first month, two months, you will remember every day," she says. "Every day, every morning—you turn around, you think about him. Like you will step on one of his things, maybe his jacket, and you will remember. You will see his picture on the wall, and you will remember. It's the only thing you have in your head," she continues. "So, that's how it is."

Now, eight months later, these thoughts have begun to subside somewhat. "But as time goes by," Marie states, "you start to forget. In six months, eight months—you probably will spend a day without remembering."

Megan and Kristen have both found the second year after the death to be more difficult. Megan's mother died a year and a half ago. "I had a year of being really numb," she says. "I just wanted to avoid the whole thing and I had a really tough time talking about it." The second year was very different. "And then the following year, that's all I wanted to do was to talk about it and just cry."

It's been a year and ten months since Kristen's father had a heart attack. "My father died and I was upset and it bothered me for about six months, until about June. I was perfectly fine until November rolled around and then I was really depressed again until June."

The second round of depression was much harder to handle, however. "When my father first died, he died and it was over and that was that," Kristen explains. "But when my father died again [speaking of the second period of pain], it lasted longer because he'd already been dead and it wasn't like he died and it was over."

Gary is somewhat of an exception. While others may also have blocked some of their emotions in an effort to fend off the pain, Gary has made a concentrated effort to be stoical, to feel nothing at all. Even so, two years after his father's death, there are some signs that he too may be starting to let some of his feelings in. "Lately, since the beginning of summer, I started to express when I'm happy, when I'm feeling good, more. But I'm still keeping my bad feelings inside," he states.

When Julie looks back on the three years since her brother's death, she can see the different stages she's passed through. "The first one is shock and you don't really want to accept it," she recalls. "Everything seems like a dream. And it's really hard—it's almost like you feel guilty for not feeling sad. Then time goes by and you start to really miss them. I guess you get depressed, 'cause it's been a while and you finally start to realize it's for real. And you really miss the person."

The acute pain is gone, but now, as Julie says, it's hard for other reasons. "It's been a long time, it's been three years. And it's almost like the memories are starting to slip. More than they did. And it's harder to remember and that gets you angry!" she adds.

While it's true that the pain lessens with time, it still returns periodically. "I would have said five years was a long time," Abby comments. "Five years is not a long time. I can just walk around one morning, like when I've just woken up, and feel like I'm going to start to cry." The pain is different now, though.

"It's a much more settled pain. It's something I'm used to," she adds.

Even now, however, there are times when her brother's death seems like a bad dream. "Reality is a very strange, weird thing," Abby states. "It just really flips me out daily. Because sometimes I still walk around saying, 'I can't believe it! I can't believe I'll never see Ben again.'"

It's been ten years since Brenda's brother and Elaine's best friend died. Now in their early twenties, these young women look back on their experience. "As time passes, you just become used to it, that it happened," Brenda says. "You don't think about it as much as when it first happened. Now I can go quite a long time without thinking about it, until I see something or someone he dated, a picture of him. So, I guess you become used to what happened."

It took Elaine a long time to deal with Mandy's death. "Me and my friends," she remembers, "we didn't talk about it, really. We talked about her on her birthday. We talked about it on the day that she died a year later. But other than that, we really didn't talk about her for a good couple of years. I guess we were just more able to deal with it at that point. We felt a little more removed from the situation. I think it was too hard for us at the time when she died. Maybe our denial lasted a long time," she concludes, thoughtfully.

Part Two
The Initial Period

FOR MANY of the adolescents who participated in writing this book, the effort to cope with the death of someone close began well before the person in question actually died. These young people knew that a friend or family member was terminally ill and would soon die. For others, death struck unexpectedly and the process of grieving began when they learned that someone they cared about had died.

Obviously, these two situations differ in important aspects. Nevertheless, in some respects, it seems not to matter whether there was advance warning of the death or not. In both cases, it often seems completely unreal and unbelievable to many adolescents that someone so important to them could actually die.

Perhaps because the enormity of their loss is far too much for many bereaved teenagers to face initially, the period surrounding the death is usually marked by denial, shock, and depression. These responses serve to dampen painful and overwhelming emotions to a level where they can be tolerated, allowing bereaved adolescents to regain the necessary strength to deal with their devastating feelings later on.

While adults may react similarly to the death of someone they love, in their case this protective numbing is generally short-lived. Adolescents, with their greater vulnerability, seem to need a much longer period, sometimes up to a year, to recuperate before attempting to deal with the emotional reality of the death.

Two events within this initial period, however, force bereaved adolescents to begin the process of facing their loss head on: the funeral and returning to school.

2 / Before the Death

*I walked out of the hospital and I said to my
mother, "Is she going to die?" And my mother
said, "Probably." And I said, "Well, then we're
just going to have to pray for a miracle!" Fantasy
sort of stuff.*—ELAINE

*I know you have preparation, but it doesn't sink
in. You keep putting it off, saying, 'It won't
happen.'*—VICKY

IT CAME as a shock to Terry when her mother died,
although logically, it shouldn't have. For two years,
both she and her younger sister, Stephanie, had
known their mother had cancer. And they'd seen the
effects of it on her body—first there was the loss of
her hair, then the constant throwing up, the terrible
headaches, the lumps that appeared everywhere.

Finally, a week before she died, their mother went
into a coma. "Even then," says Terry, "I still kept
thinking, you know, 'She'll get better!'"

Like Terry and Stephanie, many of the other bereaved adolescents whose experiences are presented
here lost someone as a result of a long-term illness.

In almost all of these cases, the signs pointed unequivocally to the fact that the illness was terminal. Yet, when death finally came, it was usually a shock.

Events that occur before a death—and the way the teenagers involved respond to them—influence how adolescents cope with the death afterwards. In most cases, denial is a major way of coping during the painful and stressful time of a terminal illness.

There are many good reasons why people of any age deny the possibility that someone they love is dying. The fact may simply be too frightening to accept. Denying it buys time, giving the person a chance to examine the information little by little in smaller, less threatening pieces. As Vicky says, "In the back of my head, I said, 'My mom's not going to die.' But I was thinking about the fact. Maybe I wasn't accepting it, but I was thinking it."

Like most people, adolescents feel ambivalent about being told upsetting but important facts. Julie wanted to face the truth—almost as much as she didn't. Although she was aware that her younger brother had cancer and was getting worse, it never occurred to Julie that he might die. While she was staying with relatives, however, a cousin matter-of-factly told her that he wasn't expected to survive.

"That really hit me hard!" Julie recalls. "I remember it very clearly because it was the first time that I really thought about it. We went to bed and after my cousin fell asleep, I started to cry."

Her parents were out for the evening with her aunt and uncle, so Julie got up and quietly paced the house, waiting for them to return so she could ask them if what she'd heard was true. "I remember just looking out the window, waiting for them to come home," she says. "Thoughts went through my mind of what it would be like, you know, without him."

But when her parents finally walked through the door, Julie couldn't bring herself to ask them. "I lost my nerve," she says, softly. "I said I wanted a drink of water and I went back upstairs."

While the possibility of death may be too frightening to face, the reality of the illness itself may be just as difficult to deal with. Except for Kristen, the twelve young people who lost someone as a result of long-term illnesses lost them to particularly ravaging diseases—diseases that slowly transformed the people they loved into pain-ridden shadows.

Adults frequently find themselves unable to cope in these circumstances, so it's little wonder that adolescents also need to avoid these situations at times. Unfortunately, that almost always means avoiding the sick person, something they often feel great guilt over later.

Erica's reaction to seeing her stepmother right before death was not unusual—she fled. "It was really, really awful!" Erica remembers painfully. "It was just *too much*! She was on dialysis, you know—all these tubes in her. And we're clapping in her face and she doesn't know who we are and my uncle's meditating over her. We had a Ouija board so she could point to letters and she was trying to write, and it was just *freaky*!"

It's hard for any of us to face difficult and painful emotions and harder still to face the possibility that we may soon lose a person we love. In addition to these reasons for denial, however, adolescents experience some special pressures to ignore the reality that a parent is dying. This is the period in their lives when teenagers are normally breaking away from their families, not drawing closer. But moving away from the family can be scary, and teenagers also want to feel sure that their parents will be there if needed.

Having a parent become critically ill completely disrupts this process. Not only is the sense of security shattered, but the teenager feels a desire to grab onto, not push away from, the dying parent. Frequently, adolescents resolve the conflict between what they need to do as teenagers, on the one hand, and what they want to do as children of dying parents, on the other, by denying how sick the parent really is. This allows them to behave as normal teenagers and push away from their families instead of clinging to the parent who is dying.

Megan's response was typical. When she was in the eighth grade, she found out that her mom had breast cancer. "I just thought, 'She'll have an operation and it'll be over and that will be it,'" Megan remembers. "I mean, there was this little glimmer that, 'Oh, no! She has cancer! What if she should die?' But then there was the feeling of, 'Oh, but that can't really happen.'"

Her mother's mastectomy was declared successful and Megan assumed the danger was over. But the following fall, her mother started having headaches. "I kind of knew something was going on," Megan continues. "But I didn't want to think about it."

Another complication is that, because of their age, adolescents may be asked to help in the care of the dying parent, increasing the pressure to a breaking point.

"It was really bad," Megan recalls. "She was in a lot of pain and she was taking a lot of painkillers like Demerol and other really powerful drugs. Finally, she was paralyzed. She could only just move her head a little. I mean, people had to feed her.

"And my dad would ask, 'Megan, can you help?' I'd say, 'Dad, I really can't! I've got to go out. I'm going to go with my friends.' And sometimes I feel bad that I didn't really help."

Terry needed to avoid the constant pressures of her mother's illness too. At times she just disappeared. "I tried to stay out of the house," she admits. At other times she rebelled. "Once my mother asked me to rub her head 'cause she had lots of headaches because of it, and I said, 'No! I don't want to!' and I slammed the door on her. And she started crying and stuff. . . . After it happened, I felt so guilty."

Eventually, the stress may build to such a level that the teenager just wants the situation to end—one way or the other. "It was a month and a half of coming home from school, and when normal kids would come home and play around the yard and watch TV, it was time to go to the hospital. It was watching this person just be in so much pain!" says Vicky. "In some ways, I wanted it over!" she admits. "Because every day, I'd walk in from school and, well, you hesitate before you open the door. 'Is it going to happen today? Am I going to walk in there and are they going to tell me, "Well, she's gone."

"You just get so sick of the waiting and the waiting! And the pain!" Vicky continues. "You just think, 'I want this out of my life!' Not, 'I want this *person* out of my life,' because you love them so much. But you just—"

These feelings are natural and normal. The problem arises when, in their need to deny the seriousness of the disease or to push away the pain, adolescents behave toward the sick person in ways that are unkind and that they later regret. Their feelings and actions may be completely understandable, but that doesn't stop them from feeling guilty.

Yet the period before the person dies is also a time of opportunity. Although most of the teenagers here express some regret concerning their responses then, many also feel good about some of the things they did—emotions they were able to convey, support they were able to give. Kristen is one of these fortunate kids.

"See, every time we talked on the phone, he'd say, 'I love you, Kristen,' and I'd say, 'Yeah, Dad, bye,' and hang up. I never said I loved him because it was what he wanted me to say," Kristen explains. "And I didn't feel like being pressured into saying something, you know, that he wanted me to say."

But for some reason, she responded differently before leaving on vacation. "The last time I ever talked to him, we were on the phone and he said, 'I love you, Kristen,' and I said, 'I love you too, Dad,' and then I hung up. That I said that really made me happy!" Kristen says, smiling. "Because even though he died and I didn't get to talk to him again, I told my father that I loved him."

For Stephanie, the last five months of her mother's life were very special. Unlike her older sister, Terry, Stephanie was just entering adolescence at the time and hadn't really begun to break away from her parents. On the contrary, Stephanie wanted to get as close to her mother as possible. "I was really scared I was going to lose her," Stephanie says, "because I really needed her."

She found her mother's physical deterioration as difficult to tolerate as her older sister did, but because Stephanie was experiencing different pressures, she was able to be there more consistently for her mother. "That was our closest period," she recalls fondly.

The day she and her father helped her mother buy a wig is one of her favorite memories. "The salesman was being really silly," Stephanie remembers. "He kept putting all these ridiculous wigs on her and we were all just laughing and laughing! When we got home, my mom hugged me and said, 'Thanks a lot for coming!' I think it meant a lot to her that I went," she adds with a smile.

Although Stephanie did some things during this period that she regrets, she can look back on many times when she was able to be supportive to her mother—times that brought them closer together then and provided memories that comfort her now.

Megan's ability to talk with her mother during this time not only brought them even closer but helped her face reality. "It was just really weird," Megan says. "Some days, my mom would look fabulous! She'd be really lively and she'd be in a good mood and she wouldn't throw up. And I'd think, 'She's getting better. OK, this is over! It's clearing.'"

But these periods were always short-lived. Each time the symptoms returned, they were worse than before. "People say I was denying," Megan recalls, "but seriously, I thought she wasn't going to die. My aunt kept saying, 'Megan, you've got to face it! Look at her!' And I thought, 'You don't know her! *I* know her!'"

The facts were becoming harder and harder to ignore, however. Finally, Megan's pain and confusion were just too much for her to handle alone. "One night, I just couldn't deal with it anymore. I went down and I said, 'Mom, I've got to talk to you. Listen, I really don't want you to go. I'm going to miss you so much. It's really painful to watch you.'

"It was one of her good nights," Megan continues, "and she said, 'You know, I really understand. I'm sorry I'm doing this, but I'm not going to live. I'm truly sorry. . . . You're my best friend.'"

They talked for two hours. "It helped me a lot to talk to my mother about it," Megan says. "She was the only one who knew what was going on, who would be honest with me." It seems that others tried to tell Megan the truth too. But her mother was clearly the one she needed to hear it from.

3 / When Death Strikes

Well, you won't believe this—I started laughing.
—MARIE

I kind of blanked out then and until the next day I really don't remember anything. I don't remember leaving the hospital, getting home, going to bed.—BRENDA

REGARDLESS of how or when it happens, it's always hard to believe. Marie's father finally succumbed after a long and visibly painful battle with cancer, while Brenda's brother was struck out of the blue by a speeding car. Yet both girls went into shock when the person they cared about died.

Shock is a normal defense against the devastation that can result from an emotionally traumatic event. To protect us against overwhelming pain, the body and mind shut down, placing us on a kind of automatic pilot. By insulating us from physical and emotional pain, shock helps buy us time in which to adjust to a new and terrible reality. Yet, because this protective insulation separates us from our feelings, people in shock often behave in ways that, under other circumstances, would seem inappropriate.

Marie had known for months that her father's illness was fatal. He'd told her so. And even if he hadn't, Marie wasn't blind. His condition had deteriorated so much that it was surprising he was still alive. But when the call came from the hospital, the news of his death hit her like a slap in the face.

To her amazement, Marie's first response was to laugh, though she certainly didn't think the situation was funny. Needless to say, this behavior seemed very strange to her. Although she didn't know it at the time, Marie was relieved to learn later that unusual emotional reactions like this are actually quite common for someone in shock.

"Then I got up, went to the bathroom, back to the living room, and sat down," Marie recalls. "My mother was still crying. And that's when I started *crying!*"

Like many people, Marie reacted physically as well as emotionally to the shock of her father's death. "Then I got a headache, I couldn't eat. I don't know, I was sick," she continues. "I didn't know what I was . . . what I was doing. I just stayed there. People were talking to me but I couldn't hear what they were saying."

Brenda had no advance warning of her brother's death. She had just returned from an outing when the hospital called, saying that he had been struck by a car. Although Larry was in critical condition, the fact that he might die never occurred to her. On the way to the hospital, Brenda's mother kept saying, "He's not going to make it. I know he's not going to make it." But that just didn't seem possible to Brenda.

"I couldn't *think* of something like that happening to him," she says.

While on the operating table, however, Larry died. "I was in shock, I think," Brenda recalls. "From leaving the hospital to the next morning is just a blank. I can't remember it at all! I have no idea what happened."

Like Marie, Brenda didn't respond at first as one might expect—she didn't cry. But then, to Brenda, the whole situation seemed completely unreal. "It was hard to believe my brother had died," she explains. "I couldn't believe that had happened! I didn't really cry for him," she adds. "I can remember not really crying until later on."

Erica's entire family expected her stepmother, Sharon, to die. Relatives had raced to her bedside from all over the country just to be there during the last days of her life. Although the circumstances surrounding her death were very different from the way Larry died, Erica's reactions sound a lot like Brenda's.

"I couldn't cry," Erica says. "I was just walking around, thinking, 'I know I should be crying but I'm not.'" Like Marie, she couldn't sit still. "I was just walking around, pacing around. I couldn't sit down, I couldn't do anything. I didn't really understand that Sharon was gone," she adds.

Erica's inability to cry, to feel sad the way she thought she was supposed to, really bothered her. "The worst thing is that I went and picked my sister up that night. She came in on the boat and we went up to the marina and watched this comedy show," she admits. "We're laughing, having a good time, and all this time in the back of my mind, I'm thinking, 'We shouldn't be having a good time. We should be grieving, we should be sad.'"

Kristen was more than sad, she was devastated. But she found her own reactions confusing too. "My stepmother's sister called," she recalls. "I answered the phone and she wanted to talk to my mom, who wasn't there. So she talked to my aunt Laura. And when she didn't want to talk to me, I knew my father had died. Nobody told me but I just knew.

"I got hysterical and I started crying," Kristen continues. But for some strange reason, the tears stopped. "And then, I didn't know what to do because I stopped crying. I felt bad that I wasn't crying. I felt like everybody was sitting on top of me and I was thinking, 'What do I do?' So I just sat there."

Abby was completely traumatized by the news that her brother had died in an accident. "The morning of his death, I was in bed sleeping and I heard my other brother screaming, 'Ben's dead! Ben's dead!' It really flipped me out! That's a horrible, scary, freaky, frightening thing to wake up to!"

In addition to being hurt, angry, and confused, Abby got very ill. "I remember, I got *so* sick, physically ill, I mean. I was in bed for twenty-four hours."

In some cases, the initial shock and sense of unreality linger longer than usual because the person is trying very hard not to face painful feelings. Gary is one of these people. "After he died, it's been like there's no reality, my life is all a dream," he says, speaking of his father's sudden death. "It just doesn't seem real. It's just an event that you go through."

One of the reasons it doesn't seem real is because Gary doesn't want it to feel real—it hurts too much. In fact, Gary would prefer not to feel much of anything. "There's a group of characters in there," he says, referring to one of his favorite books, "whose mode of life is stoic, to show nothing. And I try to model myself after that. I try, if I'm getting mad, to just keep it in." Unfortunately, Gary feels guilty when he's happy because he knows his mother is suffering, so he stifles good feelings as well.

But burying feelings doesn't make them go away. Gary's reaction upon hearing that a friend's mother died recently is a good clue to the shock and pain he felt, and feels, about his own situation. "When I found out his mother died," Gary says, "I was in French class and I almost literally got sick. I had to be excused from class." What made the news so upsetting? "It was like a flashback," he explains, "of what he must be going through. I just went home and crashed, went to sleep."

Although reactions of shock are very common, even when death is expected, not all teenagers respond that way. Jay had a sense that his sister might die when she did. "When I left for school," he recalls, "she was breathing really hard and she couldn't move, and it was really scary. So I came to school just knowing that today was the day."

When the principal asked his teacher to send him to the office, Jay knew why. "I thought, 'Oh wow! There it goes! It happened.' I just stood up in class and swore. Then I walked out into the lobby and my dad was there. We got in the car, and he said,

'Carrie died this morning.' And I said, 'I know.' And then I started to cry."

Even for Jay, however, there were moments when things took on a dreamlike quality. "It was weird," he says, remembering what it was like when he got home. "My mom was leaning against the sliding door. And it looked sort of like a picture, like a cover of a book. It was funny, because we just sat there and nobody talked for about half an hour."

Like Jay, Megan had a premonition that her mother was going to die that day. "She had a really bad night, and that morning I woke up and I had this funny feeling. It was really bizarre. I was in the shower and I had such a strong sense of, 'You should really stay home today.'"

So Megan wasn't surprised when her brother came to school to get her. On the way home, she recalls, "I had all these visions, like, 'What's going to be at the house? Is she dead yet? Is there going to be an ambulance?' I was really scared!"

When she and her brother arrived, her mother had just died. As Megan remembers it, the scene was all too real. "The worst part—this still haunts me— they came and they took her body. They covered it with a blanket. They just kind of . . . it looked like she was just kind of thrown. . . . The hardest thing was to watch them drive out of the driveway. And take my mother away."

However, Megan had many moments later on when it didn't seem possible that her mother had died. Truly accepting the fact that the person is actually gone and gone forever takes a long time. Yet even for those most in shock, the unbelievable eventually becomes believable. For most bereaved adolescents, the process of accepting the reality of the death begins with the funeral.

4 / The Funeral

The day we had the memorial service . . . I hadn't cried at all and then that day, I just broke down. I realized she wasn't on vacation, she was gone!—ERICA

I wasn't upset during the funeral because I was prepared for it. But when they lowered her into the ground, then I knew, "This is it! I'm never going to see her again!" That's when I started crying.—STEPHANIE

F OR MANY, the period surrounding the death itself is a confusing blur. Numb with shock, most bereaved adolescents, like most adults, have difficulty fully grasping what's happened. Although they are aware intellectually that the person has died, on an emotional level the death may seem completely unreal. Often, the first glimmer of what the death truly means is the funeral—with its unmistakable message of finality.

Although most people find it difficult to attend a funeral, this service can be an important part of coming to terms with the death. Regardless of the many variations in funeral rites, they all serve to help us acknowledge the death and say a final farewell. In this country, religious funerals are usually either Christian or Jewish.

Many Christian funerals are preceded by a wake at the funeral home. Held a few days after the death, the wake gives friends a chance to meet informally with the bereaved family, share memories of the person who died, and offer consolation to each other. The funeral itself takes place a few days later at the church. After the funeral service, those who wish may follow the family to the cemetery for the burial.

In the Jewish tradition, the funeral service is held within a day or two after death at the temple or, more commonly, the funeral home. Unlike Christian funerals, flowers are not customary at Jewish services. For seven days following the funeral, many Jewish families observe *shiva*, a period of mourning when the family receives friends who wish to offer condolences. Finally, eleven months after the burial, the grave marker is unveiled in a ritual at the cemetery.

Seeing the body of a person they loved can be particularly hard for adolescents. If the body has not been cremated, the funeral or wake is when mourners may actually view the corpse, and this experience is often part of what makes the funeral so difficult.

Julie's case was a little different, however. She had already seen her brother's body at home, shortly after he died. Toward the end of his illness, when it was apparent that there was nothing the doctors could do for him, Julie's parents had brought the child home. When he died, they woke her and took her into his bedroom. "It looked like he was sleeping," Julie remembers. "And that's how I wanted it to be. That's how my mind saw it, I guess, because that's how I wanted it.

"But what was really hard was the wake," she adds. It was much more difficult to imagine her brother was asleep when he was lying in a casket. "I thought I was going to be able to handle it. But when I saw him, I just burst into tears. It kind of scared me to see him like that! That's when it first hit me."

For others, it's just too painful to have to confront the fact that the person they loved is a corpse. "I didn't go in," says Marie, referring to her father's wake. "I got to the door and I stepped back into the hallway. I just couldn't look at him. It would have been too painful to me. So, I just said, 'No! I won't do any of it.' I just sat there and cried," she adds. "Then I went back home."

Often, it isn't just a matter of wishing to avoid the pain of dealing with the death. Lynette and Marie both worried that the sight of their father's body would drive out memories of him when he was alive, memories they wanted to hold onto. "I wish I hadn't gone to the funeral home. I wish I didn't see him dead," Lynette says. "I wish I had the memory of how he was alive." Her sister agrees. "That's why I didn't want to look at him," Marie recalls. "I knew that in my dreams I would see him . . . his face . . . lying there."

Adults can feel this way too. Brenda's parents wanted to preserve the memory of her brother when he was alive. "The casket was closed," Brenda says. "My mother wanted that. Since he was a model, he had a big portfolio. They had his portfolio next to the casket so if people wanted to see what he looked like, they could look at that instead of looking at him dead." Brenda is glad her parents handled it this way. "I think if I saw him dead, that's all I'd ever picture is him dead."

But not seeing his body, Brenda thinks, has made it harder to accept the reality of her brother's death. Even now, ten years later, she says, "I *still* think that it's all a joke sometimes, that he just wanted to get away or something. Because I never saw the body."

For many bereaved adolescents, the wake or the funeral is the first time it begins to register that the loss is permanent. "Now, I knew my mother was gone and I knew she wasn't going to be there," Vicky explains. "But the thing I was having the most difficulty grasping was the fact that she was not going to be there when I graduated from high school or when I got married. I couldn't see her not being there in the future.

"I could accept the fact that she was gone," Vicky continues, "but I was having a terrible time accepting the fact that she wasn't coming back. And that didn't really occur to me until the day of the wake."

Erica knew her stepmother, Sharon, had died. But somehow she kept expecting her to return. It wasn't until the funeral that it began to dawn on her what had actually happened. "Here's this man talking about her and that means she's *gone!*" Erica recalls. "That's *it*! She's gone and she's not coming back!"

The realization hit her like a ton of bricks. "I was the only one who was affected like that," Erica remembers. "No one else in the family was—I mean, I cried for two or three hours."

On the other hand, sometimes the sense of loss fades temporarily just when one would least expect it to—on the day of the funeral. After the services, friends and relatives came over to Terry and Stephanie's house. Somehow, the girls and their cousins got involved in a soccer game. "Everyone was looking at us like we were crazy," Terry remembers. "Even my dad."

Terry thought her behavior was a little strange too. "It seems crazy, you know," she says. "I pictured myself just freaking out in the house and here I was laughing with all my friends and just talking about it. We were supposed to be crying, but it didn't bother me," she admits with surprise. "My dad was all misty, but I honestly had a *good* time!"

Other bereaved adolescents find the funeral too much to handle. Gary was trying to block out the pain, not ask for more. His father had been cremated, so Gary didn't have to view the body. If he'd had his way, he wouldn't have gone to the memorial service either. "For a long time, I just wanted to get out of there," he recalls. "I really didn't want to be there. It reminded me again."

In spite of the pain they know they'll feel, however, most bereaved teenagers choose to attend the funeral or memorial service. They usually want to be there with the rest of their family or, if the person who died was a friend, with the rest of their friends. They may think they should go and that they'll feel guilty if they don't. But perhaps most important, they recognize it's a chance to say goodby and a step in coming to grips with their loss. "I guess it was the last time," Lynette says, "so I wanted to be there." "I think I thought if I went, it would help me accept it," Julie recalls. "It did help."

Once at the funeral, however, unanticipated events can occur that are difficult to handle. The emotions of relatives, in particular, can be unnerving, especially if they are unexpected. Kristen's older sister is a controlled woman who rarely expresses emotions. Thus, Kristen was completely thrown by her reaction at their father's funeral.

"At my father's memorial service," she remembers, "she came over and started crying on my shoulder. I'd never seen my sister cry in my whole life. I'd never seen my sister be angry. I thought, 'Stop! I don't know what to do!' "

Adam's parents' reactions were more than unexpected, they were down-right frightening. Upon seeing the temple packed with his brother's friends, his parents fell apart. "I've never seen my parents like that," Adam says. "It was pretty scary! I mean, I didn't know what to do about it but I was upset that they had to go through that!"

Funerals are important not only because they provide a chance to say a final goodby to the person who has died and to begin to accept the reality of the death. They also provide an opportunity to acknowledge the importance of the person's life and to recognize the relationships others have had with that person. When these relationships have become complicated by divorce and/or remarriage, the funeral service can become an emotional mine field.

When the priest asked the close relatives to shake everyone's hand as the congregation left her father's funeral, Kristen found herself in a very awkward situation. "The priest didn't know my brothers and sister because they're much older than me and they don't go to church," she explains. "When nobody moved, he took my stepmother and me, which made me really uncomfortable because she doesn't get along with my brothers and sister, and I'd rather be with them than with her. So anyway, I had to go and shake hands. And that made my sister even more upset, because she was totally overlooked as a member of the family and wasn't invited to go and stand there and shake everybody's hand."

Kristen also worried that her mother, who was her father's ex-wife, would be placed in a position beneath her stepmother. To Kristen's relief, it wasn't that bad. "The friends that my father had made during my stepmother's period didn't go, because they were just business associates. But the friends my father had known during my mom's period, they were all there," she says. "So that made me happy because then my mom was ahead of my stepmother—she knew everybody."

While the funeral was difficult for Kristen because her sister's and mother's relationships with her father were not given enough importance, Pam's experience was the opposite. Technically, Pam was not a member of her boyfriend's family, but they treated her as if she were. And the fact that everyone acknowledged how important her relationship with Brian had been made the funeral a very positive event for her.

"It was very special to me because of the way his parents treated me. They treated me like I was his wife," Pam says. "I was in the receiving line and there was a section of the liturgy that was dedicated to me. And I was the first person behind the coffin when you go up the aisle."

Others also recognized how much Brian had cared for her, and that was important. "The priest who did the funeral mass was a young guy and he was torn up by this whole situation," she adds. "The night before the funeral, he couldn't sleep so he ended up making out these little cards with what he thought Brian was saying to his family. And he made a card for me."

Knowing that Brian's death mattered, not just to his family and to her, but to other people as well, was important to Pam. And the funeral was a very tangible demonstration of the love others felt for him. When she got up to leave, "The church was full, and people were standing against the back and in the outer lobby and there were even people standing outside of the church because they couldn't fit in. It felt so good to turn around and see that—to know that Brian knew so many people and that so many people cared!"

5 / *Going Back to School*

Part of my fear was that something would happen, somebody would say something that would really throw me. And I would just be all alone, flipped out by myself.—ABBY

No one talked to me about it . . . at all. I felt kind of like an outsider at school because no one said anything about it.—JULIE

UNLESS the death occurs during summer vacation, bereaved adolescents must return to school soon after the funeral. Many find this prospect terrifying—and with good reason. For most of these young people, the death has been the most traumatic event of their lives. Coping with it in the sheltered privacy of the family has been difficult enough. Now, precisely at the time when they feel least in control of themselves and their lives, they are required to deal with this painful situation in full view of their peers.

In a society with few clear guidelines for managing the social aspects of grief, bereaved teenagers feel especially lost when it comes to handling the death in public. They have no idea of what to expect or how to respond to their classmates' reactions. Abby's panic was typical.

"Oh, no!" she thought. "I have to talk to these people. They're going to say they're sorry, they're going to say the wrong thing, they're not going to say anything. They're going to look at me and pretend I don't exist because they're not going to know what to say so they're not going to talk to me."

Unfortunately, these fears are well founded. Like the grieving adolescents, the teenagers who are their classmates are ill equipped to negotiate this difficult terrain. Not knowing what to do, they all too frequently do nothing.

"All I can remember," says Brenda, "is kids just staring at me, whispering about what happened to my brother. Nobody would really talk to me about it. And when *I* talked about it, they got really nervous. They didn't want to talk about it. It was just too scary for them to talk about."

Julie's classmates carefully avoided mentioning her brother's death. Although her teacher had informed everyone of what had happened, no one said anything to her. In fact, no one said anything at all. "I remember walking in," she says, "and everything was quiet."

How did this make her feel? "Half and half," she replies. On the one hand, Julie dreaded having to explain the situation to others, so her classmates' silence let her off the hook. "I was kind of relieved that I didn't have to answer any questions," she admits.

But their total lack of response left her in an even

more painful position. She couldn't tell whether her brother's death—or her grief—even mattered to them at all. "It was hard to figure out if people didn't know how to react or if they just didn't care," she says.

Even when others do manage to respond, it may not make the bereaved person feel any better. Often, this is because classmates, in their awkwardness, say things that seem insensitive. "One girl said to me," Abby recalls, "and this was really stupid, 'Sorry to hear about your brother, but I guess it must have just been his time.' Well, maybe it was his time, but you don't say that!"

The problem is complicated by the fact that some schoolmates are close friends of the bereaved teenager while others are only casual acquaintances, and it can be hard for them to know what kind of response is appropriate to make. When they misjudge, their mistakes can upset the very person they're trying to console. A too-distant response from a close friend, for example, can be painfully disappointing, while a too-intimate response from a mere acquaintance is often enraging.

"I stayed out for about a week and when I came back to school, everyone acted totally fake," says Megan angrily. "People I was never really friends with came up to me and hugged me!" Stephanie immediately threw out the sympathy cards she received from kids at school. "It was garbage!" she says. "People I barely knew were writing me all this stuff, like 'I can't believe this is happening . . . I'm always here for you.'"

At other times, responses from classmates seem

uncaring because, in fact, they are. Many people in school are not friends of the bereaved and are not particularly concerned about his or her feelings. To them, the death is a hot conversation item, to be treated like any other piece of gossip. Handling interactions with people like this is difficult for anyone. It's especially hard for a grief-stricken adolescent.

Megan remembers such an instance. "There's a girl I've known since first grade all the way up to high school and we haven't talked since first grade. She called me and said, 'What happened?' You know, the whole thing. And she was acting really supportive and then she never called again after I told her the whole story. She just wanted to find out the inside scoop." Needless to say, Megan felt used.

Terry and Stephanie had a similar experience when their mother died. "Some girls came up and said the rudest things I've ever heard!" Terry says. "Asking if it was an open coffin, you know, and I don't even know the girl! Asking, 'Did you have to kiss her after she was dead?'"

"It's the gossips," Stephanie adds, "that want to say, 'Oh, I'm good friends with her and she told me all this stuff.' Just to get the word around, because everyone's asking, 'What happened? What happened?'"

Gary's experience was even more unpleasant. He sees himself as a person with little self-confidence and few friends, and he didn't expect much support from classmates. "No one really said anything. I wasn't expecting anyone to because I wasn't on good terms with that many people there. The friends I had

said they were sorry and asked if there was anything they could do. But they just carried on regular
business."

But neither was he expecting a hostile attack.
"Two weeks after my father died, I had soccer practice," Gary adds. "This is one of the main reasons I
dropped off the team—I was just fooling around with
a few kids and I goofed up the kick or something.
And one of them said, sort of behind my back but
like he wanted me to hear it, 'Oh, poor Gary, his
father died. Awww.'" It's hard to know why people
would do cruel things like this, but it sometimes happens. Perhaps such behavior is a way of covering up
the fear that the same thing might happen to them.

On the bright side, when friends offer support, it
can make a big difference in getting through that
first awful day back at school. "Denise picked me
up for school and she held my hand from the parking
lot to the school," Abby recalls fondly. "She brought
me to my locker. That whole day, she held my hand
in the hallway. Which, when you're a senior in high
school, well, girls just don't hold hands!" Abby adds,
"She held my hand to every single class. And she
made it all right!"

Most bereaved teenagers have their hands full just
responding to their peers' reactions. Occasionally,
however, a young person is actually able to take
charge of the situation and tell classmates how to
treat him. After his sister died, the kids in Jay's class
fell all over themselves in an effort to help him. Jay
hated it!

"They all started to baby me, you know? 'Oh, I'll

sharpen your pencil, here you go. Oh, I'll give you help on this.' And so during class, I stood up and said, 'Stop it! I'm not a baby. I can handle it. It's my life. Just don't baby me anymore. I'll be fine!' From then on it was fine," he adds.

It was critical to Jay that his friends not treat him differently. "Sometimes, when somebody dies in the family, you can become the oddball of the school. You could act different or whatever—it's strange," he explains. "I didn't act different. The first day I came back, when I stood up and told the class what I wanted, everyone treated me that way. And so I acted like my old self."

It's primarily this fear of being seen as "different," of being cut off and isolated from others, that makes returning to school so hard for most bereaved teenagers. Although the prospect of not belonging is upsetting to any adolescent, it's especially terrifying to a young person whose sense of security has just been ripped apart by the death of someone close.

"I didn't want people to think I was different," Abby says, echoing the thoughts of most teenagers in her situation. Yet on some level, Abby knew that was impossible. After all, she *was* different now. "There's no way that people can *not* think you're different, at least for a little while," she adds softly. "Because something major and tragic has happened."

The fear of being seen as different can express itself in many ways. In Adam's case, he thought others expected him to lose control or behave strangely. "I was kind of scared [of returning to school]. I thought,

'OK, I'm going to get there and everyone's going to be looking at me—wondering, waiting for me to break down.' "

Megan worried about how others would see her too. "I was really scared to go back to school. I felt that people were going to think I was different now and treat me differently." Like Abby, Megan *felt* different now, but she focused on the perception that her mother's death had made her family half a family—and herself less a person. "Yeah, I felt a lot different. I felt that I was nothing anymore. I felt kind of like an orphan, like I wasn't worthy, that now my friends who had both their mother and father were better." In a culture that still attaches a stigma to "broken" families and death, it's not surprising that Megan, who experienced both, felt somehow tainted.

Although it can be difficult, it's important for bereaved teenagers to return to their normal world after the death and, for most adolescents, this means school. There are some things that friends and classmates can do, however, to make this transition a little less upsetting. "I think now," says Julie, "though I didn't at the time, that it would have been easier if they'd talked about it a little bit to me. I felt I was an outsider at school because no one ever said anything about it."

Looking back on an awkward remark that angered her at the time, Abby agrees. "But then again, at least she made an effort, and she said something and that was nice. I would rather somebody say something than to just blow me off or pretend nothing happened! Because at least when they say something, you know it's coming from a place where they mean it. As opposed to just denying it or thinking, 'Oh, I can't deal with this at all.' "

Efforts, however clumsy, that show schoolmates realize something terrible has happened and that they care are very important to a young person struggling to cope with a death. For it is only through these responses that bereaved teenagers can tell they still matter to their peers, that they are still a part of the group.

6 / Depression

It's as if things get done, things take care of themselves, but you're not participating. Your body is participating in your life, but you, upstairs, are just completely fried.—ABBY

I guess I was always depressed, but not that I showed it, you know. And I think that's what my parents were afraid of—that I wasn't showing it enough.—ADAM

FOR SOME adolescents, life may seem strangely suspended for months after the loss of a family member or close friend. The initial shock has passed and the death itself no longer seems completely unreal. Intellectually, the fact has registered. But neither the death nor the teenager's life seems completely real either.

To varying degrees, these bereaved adolescents are experiencing depression—not just the sad, down, or blue emotions we generally mean by the word "depressed," but a combination of specific feelings, thoughts, and behaviors that mental health professionals use to define the term. Used in this way, depression means an emotional reaction to loss which may include some or all of the following: fears and feelings of sadness; difficulty concentrating; changes in appetite or sleep patterns; lack of energy; and fantasies of death or suicidal thoughts. Suicidal feelings are not always obvious, either to the person experiencing them or to others. But they may appear in a disguised form, such as getting into accidents or taking unusual risks. Kristen describes her depression in the following way.

"It was weird," she recalls. "I'd get up at six o'clock in the morning and take my shower. . . . Actually, I didn't," she corrects herself. "My mom would have to remind me to clean my nails and to take my shower, 'cause I didn't think of appearances, I just got dressed automatically. I was so absorbed within myself that I didn't care what I looked like."

Abby had the same trouble dealing with just getting up and dressed—sometimes it didn't even occur to her that she should. "You resume your daily habits of waking up, which by the way can be a very difficult thing to do," she explains. "Something as easy as getting up, brushing your teeth, taking a shower, and getting dressed can be an effort. That can be a whole day affair.

"You can find yourself spending your entire day in your pajamas," Abby continues. "And your hair is rumpled and you haven't thought about what you're doing. But you've got to start to take care of yourself because everyone else is so busy."

Like denial and shock, depression is a way of shutting down the emotional system so that it doesn't suffer dangerous overload. When emotions shut down, however, the person may feel almost nothing at all.

"I was never tired, I was never hungry, I was never anything," Kristen says. "I had no emotion or feeling, like pain or anything."

On the surface, these adolescents are able to function, but there's often a robotlike quality to their lives. "I remember the second year better than I remember when he first died," says Kristen, "because I don't think I was really *there*." Much of this period is a blank for Abby too. "I feel like I must have been a burnt-out waste product in high school," she adds, "because there seem to be *years* of my life that I don't remember."

Brenda's description of this period is typical. "I'd come home from school and I'd sleep. I'd get up and not eat and walk the streets. I didn't want to be with anybody else. And I really don't know why I didn't want to. I didn't realize there was any kind of problem doing that."

Because they sometimes feel so little emotionally, depressed people may not know just how depressed they are. Like many young people suffering from depression, Brenda wasn't aware that anything was wrong. Kristen explains it this way. "When you're depressed, you don't think you're depressed. The first year, I didn't think I was depressed at all. I didn't feel anything, so I didn't think I was depressed. The second year, I *knew* I was depressed."

Being depressed feels a little different to each person. "I remember when my father first died," Kristen recalls, "the first year, I couldn't picture his face at all. The minute he died, I could not remember what he looked like."

Abby couldn't cry—for a long time. "Right after my brother died, I must have cried for a month straight. And then for years, I couldn't cry about *anything*! At all!" she says.

For someone like Abby, who missed the emotional release of crying and feared she would never cry again, this was a very scary development. Only in the past couple of months has this situation begun to improve. "If I'm watching a program and it's really emotional and I start to cry, I say, 'Mom, look! I'm crying! I'm crying!' " she recounts with relief.

As Abby's experience illustrates, feeling and non-feeling aren't completely separate states. Pieces of depression may linger long after the rest of the depression has lifted. Conversely, sometimes the solid wall of depression parts, letting in pain and anger, perhaps as a test to see how ready the person is to handle these emotions.

Because of the nature of depression, seriously depressed adolescents may have difficulty recognizing when they need help. Parents can see that their children are having trouble, however, and become concerned. "I was handling it almost too well," Adam recalls. "I think they were afraid I just hid everything inside." Like Kristen's and Brenda's parents, Adam's mother and father became worried enough to want him to seek professional help.

Fortunately, there are many kinds of professional counseling available to assist depressed teenagers in coping with their loss. Many churches and synagogues offer help in various ways to bereaved teenagers and adults. Some hospitals provide bereavement counseling to the survivors of patients. Community mental health clinics offer both individual and family counseling which can help everyone involved better deal with the death. Finally, support groups composed of other bereaved individuals can be especially beneficial in handling the difficult feelings that grieving people often think no one else understands.

The adolescents interviewed for this book varied in their need for the protective buffer of depression. Some were depressed for months, even a year or more. Others moved quickly from initial shock to a range of agonizing emotions. Many bounced back and forth from one to the other, feeling and then not feeling. With the possible exception of Gary, who seems to have made a conscious effort to continue blocking his feelings, all have moved or are now moving from a period of initial numbness to the next stage: a confrontation with some very painful emotions.

Part Three
When the Numbness Wears Off

LITTLE BY LITTLE, the initial denial, shock, and depression give way, exposing a range of agonizing and often conflicting feelings. Added to the usual intense and confusing emotions typical of adolescence, the pain, anger, and guilt of bereavement present grieving teenagers with a lot to handle. Just surviving their emotions can sometimes seem very difficult. But bereaved adolescents must come to understand and accept their feelings if they are to fully recover from the tremendous blow they've suffered.

Crucial to this process are the teenager's relationships with peers. Given the power—and the fragility—of adolescent friendships, it's not surprising that these relationships can be either strong sources of support or casualties of the mourning process.

The disruptions in peer relationships that can result from the added stresses of bereavement are certainly understandable. They are especially painful, however, when an adolescent's parents, because of their own grief, are unable to provide badly needed support. Fortunately, even when old friendships crumble, most bereaved teenagers manage to establish new relationships that successfully fill their needs.

7 / Pain and Anger

*I was angry! Extremely angry! But it wasn't like
I could stop myself—which I wasn't too keen
on doing. I was very happy in my anger!*

—KRISTEN

*I just want to stop having these feelings. I don't
want to be upset all the time and crying.*

—MEGAN

WHEN Abby's brother Ben died, she thought she
wouldn't be able to stand the pain. Two days after
his death, she sobbed to one of his friends, "I'm just
so unhappy! I'm so sad! I've never been so hurt in
my life! I just wish I could be normal again. When
am I going to be normal?" she asked desperately.
"When am I going to stop feeling all this pain?"

Ben's friend had unfortunately been through this
once before, and she knew something Abby could
never imagine. "She looked me in the face," Abby
recalls, "and she said, 'The pain will get worse before
it gets better.' And I didn't believe her!" Abby exclaims. "I said, 'There's no way it could get worse!
It can't be worse than this!

"You know what?" Abby adds. "It turned out that she was right. The pain got worse! Because the initial shock wears off, people stop coming to your house, and you are left . . . with yourself."

As Abby's experience illustrates, it's not that feelings of terrible hurt and unhappiness aren't there from the beginning. Even those adolescents most numbed by the initial shock have moments of excruciating pain. But as the protective layers of denial, shock, and depression slowly disappear, pain and anger surface with a new intensity.

"The pain . . . it's a weird kind of pain. You can't describe it but it *hurts*!" Abby struggles to explain. "It feels like everything inside of you is caving in."

Although these agonizing feelings may go away temporarily, they're always lurking in the background, ready to return unexpectedly. "Just the other day, we had orchestra rehearsal," Megan says. "And we were playing this piece and I started crying. And I thought, 'This is not going to start again! Please, don't tell me this is going to start again!'"

Abby agrees. "It's like a wound that won't heal," she says. "You have times when you talk and it gets better and things get better—and then there are times when the Band-Aid peels off the wound and you just can't help it."

It's hardest for Stephanie when she's alone. "When I'm in my room and no one else is home, then I'll cry. I don't cry in front of other people," she admits. "I do it when I'm alone. I guess it's 'cause I'm lonely and stuff.

"But when I'm with my friends," Stephanie says, "it keeps my mind off of it. So, when I'm alone in my room, that's when I get all depressed and I think, 'Somebody *please* call! Please call and ask me to come over!'"

Along with the pain comes a lot of anger, a feeling that is a normal part of the grieving process. "How can you not be angry," Megan asks, speaking of her mother's death, "when you lose your best friend and your mother all at once?"

It's natural for people who've lost someone they love to be furious. After all, something very terrible has happened to them. But what makes it even worse for most bereaved adolescents is that the terrible thing has happened well before it should have. Parents are not supposed to die before their children are grown. Brothers and sisters, friends, aren't supposed to die before they've had a chance to live. It isn't fair.

"Why did it happen now?" Adam asks angrily. "I mean, it doesn't seem right to say, but why not to my great-grandmother who's ninety-one and done it all? Why did it have to be him?" This made Elaine mad too. "It just seemed very unfair," she says. "Why was she taken? It should have been someone else, someone older."

Her brother's premature death not only cut his life short, it deprived Abby of the years she'd expected to spend with him. "Immediately after my brother's death, I felt really cheated!" she says. "I felt so cheated! And I still do!"

The anger at being cheated, at having to suffer unfairly, doesn't go away easily. It can't, since the cause of that anger, the actual deprivation, doesn't go away either. "Well, I'm still angry!" Marie says emphatically. "Nothing's going to change that feeling. Because it's already happened and there's nothing you can do to change it!"

Although anger after a death is normal and natural, the problem is that there's no good place to put it, no deserving target for it. Thus, it frequently spills out at anyone or anything that's handy. "In school, I kept blowing up at people," Megan recalls. "I'd yell at my brother for not walking the dog. And I'd think, 'Why am I yelling at him?'"

"I went around punching walls and stupid things like that, you know," Adam says.

Sometimes other people unwittingly provide excuses to take it out on them. "One day, I was all upset, so I asked my teacher if I could go outside. And she said yes," Jay remembers. "And there was a class out there having recess. And this kid said, 'Oh, I'm sorry about your sister.'" Jay wasn't in the mood to talk about it, but he replied, "Oh, that's OK."

But then the boy commented that his sister had looked really bad without hair. Already frayed, Jay's self-control snapped. "I lost it right there," he says. "I pulled him down and I beat him up. And I felt real good after it!"

Other people often become the focus of a bereaved person's anger. Sometimes they don't really deserve it, sometimes they do. Often it's a little of both. Kristen was very unhappy with her stepmother. "I was very mad that my father was cremated—by my stepmother," she admits. "I wanted him to be buried with a tombstone that gave him recognition that he was here in the world. Being cremated, you just disappear."

Family members, the people who are closest to adolescents and the ones most able to disappoint them, are the recipients of a lot of this anger. After her boyfriend died, Pam was furious at her mother. "I got really mad at my mom because she was the one who kept saying, 'Don't worry, everything will be fine.'"

When she first heard about the accident, Pam braced herself for Brian's death. "I had no hope whatsoever," she recalls. "The first thing that was in my head was, 'He's going to die!' But she filled my head with *hope*.

"So when I got home, and I heard that he died, I thought, 'I hate you, Mom! You're the one that made me feel better.' It was just such a waste to get up and then get down," she explains.

Elaine was very upset at her mother for not telling her how desperately ill her friend Mandy was. "I was angry about the fact that I wasn't told, that I didn't know she was dying," Elaine recalls. "You want the chance to say goodby to a person. Maybe if I had known, I would have been able to say goodby to her. So even that chance—to be able to do that—was taken away from me."

Elaine feels it was even more unfair that Mandy herself wasn't told, and she's still very angry at Mandy's parents for that. "To this day, it upsets me because I think she had a right to know that she was sick and that she was dying," Elaine says.

It hurts her to think that Mandy must have suspected that she was near death but wasn't given help and support in understanding what was going on. "She had to know something was wrong," Elaine says, "and I'm sure part of her knew she was dying. It's hard enough to know you're dying but not to be *told* that you're dying and have all these things happening to you, I think she must have been even more scared."

Marie is angry at her whole family. Since it first became obvious that her father was terminally ill, she'd wanted to talk about the situation but everyone else seemed to want to avoid the topic. "Every time I said, 'Mother, I cannot look at him anymore!,' she said, 'You just have to live with it.' Nobody wanted to talk about it!'"

When he died, it appeared to Marie that some of her siblings didn't care since they didn't show their feelings, and this made her angry. "Everyone was crying and my younger sister just stood there. I don't know what she felt, really! My other sister was crying. I know she felt sorry. But my brother, he was just . . . I don't know . . . *nothing*! He didn't cry or anything."

Ironically, her younger sister Lynette was very upset and assumes that Marie knows how much pain she felt. But because Lynette and Marie handle their grief differently, Marie is unaware of Lynette's feelings.

Marie needs to talk in order to deal with the pain, but no one else in her family can do this right now. "I thought, 'This is our father! We have to talk about what happened,' " she stresses. "But nobody wanted to talk about it."

Like family members, friends can also be sources of disappointment and anger to grieving teenagers. Frequently, this anger arises because friends don't—or can't—provide the support and solace bereaved adolescents hope for. But there are other reasons for being mad at them as well.

One of these reasons is that friends still have what the bereaved teen has lost. "I'd go over to my friends' houses and see them have a whole bunch of brothers and sisters about the same age," Julie says. "I'd watch them do things together and I'd go home and be so mad, so envious!"

Feelings of jealousy are very common and can create obstacles between the bereaved and their friends. It's even worse when friends don't appreciate what they have. "It's hard when my friends say they hate their moms," Terry states. "Like, 'Oh, I hate my mother. She's such a jerk!' That really gets to me!"

"I used to say that," Terry admits. But her perspective is different now that her mother is dead. "They're lucky to have one!" she adds sadly.

Finally, because they've had to face the fact that people they love can really die, bereaved teenagers don't treat life as lightly as most other adolescents do. Unnecessary risk-taking makes them very angry, especially if the person they lost died in an accident. Adam gets really annoyed at the casual comments of friends who get tickets for drunk driving.

"And that's all they can say about it when they were risking their lives," he says with disgust. "I don't need to hear that! But I'm not going to get up and say, 'Shut up, my brother was killed in a car!' " It makes a difference in his opinion of the person, however. "It's definitely going to make me think a little lower of them," he adds.

Perhaps the hardest person to be mad at is the one who may really deserve some anger—the person who died. "I think I was angry—this is going to sound stupid but I'm going to say it," Abby comments. "I was mad at my brother for making a stupid decision. For getting in a car when the weather was bad and he knew better."

Pam feels this even more strongly. "I think, 'Why did Brian have to have a thing for motorcycles?' He loved them! He said he wanted to *die* on his bike. The words came out of his mouth!" It's hard for Pam not to be mad at him when he did just that.

Although her father died as the result of an illness, Marie blames him for not caring enough to attend to his health. In her mind, he let himself get sick, and this makes her mad! "I thought it was his fault!" she says, because her father neglected to go for recommended check-ups to detect cancer of the prostate. When he died of this disease, she asked herself why he didn't go. "I thought he *wanted* it to happen to him!" she says. "So I was angry."

Sometimes grieving adolescents get angry at the person who died even when there's no good reason for it. Anger doesn't have to be logical. Megan watched as her mother waged a heroic battle against cancer. But when she died, Megan recalls, "I just felt really abandoned, that she didn't really care, that she didn't want to stay. I thought, 'How could she do this? Just leave me all by myself, just to fend for myself?' I went through that a lot last year."

Underneath this anger is an effort to understand how such a terrible thing could happen—both to the person who died and to the grieving people left behind. For some bereaved adolescents the ultimate responsibility and, thus, the final blame lies with God. "I remember feeling *very* angry towards God," Elaine recalls. "I thought, 'How could there be a God if he could let this happen?'"

Elaine's feelings about this have changed over the years, but Brenda's have not. "I felt resentment towards God. I hated him!" she says. "I couldn't imagine him doing this. I still feel that way. I still wonder, 'Is there really a God? If there is, why is he so bad?'"

In trying to find a reason for their pain, some teenagers come to realize that there may be no answer to the question, "Why me? Why someone I loved?" As Jay says, "You're angry about why did it have to happen to me? I mean, why couldn't it happen to some total junkie? But every time you say, 'Why did it have to happen to me?,' you have to say, 'Why *not* me?'

"I can't say, 'Well, it should have been his sister instead of my sister,'" Jay explains. "I can't say that because it *was* my sister."

8 / Guilt and Regret

*I thought something must be wrong with me,
because my dad was upset, my sister had been
crying, and I hadn't been crying.*—TERRY

*I couldn't look at her without getting sick. I felt
really bad but I couldn't. And when I went home,
I'd feel really guilty! I'd think, "You're such an
idiot! How can you do that? What if she knew
how you were feeling?"*—STEPHANIE

BECAUSE we are human beings with needs of our
own, we sometimes say angry things to people we
love or fail occasionally to be supportive of those
we care about. These behaviors are normal and part
of all healthy relationships.

When someone dies, however, bereaved friends
and family often feel guilty about past actions, wishing they had done or said things differently. Sometimes they may even feel guilty that they are still
alive, that they want to and can go back to their
usual activities. These are common feelings and it's
important to recognize and accept them as being all
right.

Although adults frequently express remorse and regret after a death, teenagers are particularly vulnerable to these emotions. As they move away from their families and begin to question the values they grew up with, adolescents subject everything and everyone to intense scrutiny. They impose exacting standards on themselves as well as on their parents and other adults. When they fail to meet their own sometimes impossible expectations, teenagers can be very hard on themselves. And when their failures can't be rectified because the people they've failed have died, these adolescents often experience crushing guilt.

Even normal feelings between siblings can be a source of guilt to an adolescent after a brother or sister has died. Julie was very fond of her aunt, although she rarely got to see her. Toward the end of her brother's life, her aunt visited Julie's family. Julie was aware that the purpose of the visit was to see her brother and that her aunt would probably never have another chance. Still, Julie felt hurt at being ignored—and felt guilty for feeling hurt.

"I think there was a part of me that was really jealous," Julie says. "And I was mad at myself for feeling that way. But, you know, I never get to see her and she was giving all her attention to him."

Realistically, parents have only so much time and energy to give, and a child who is seriously ill takes up most of it. Other children in the family must make do with what is left. They may or may not understand the reasons for this, but they always feel the deprivation. Colin had an especially hard time in this respect.

From the day his brother Jason was born, Colin had to take a back seat.

Jason suffered from a particularly severe case of cystic fibrosis. Just keeping him alive took constant effort. "Every day, there was therapeutic treatment, three times a day," Colin remembers. "And medication three times a day. Everywhere we went—" Colin's life, like the rest of his family's, revolved around Jason's medical needs. And sometimes Colin resented the attention his brother received.

When Jason died, however, Colin's parents suddenly had more time for him and his younger sister. Colin has had to adjust to getting so much attention, but he loves it! "It was different. I wasn't used to having it," he admits, "but I like it a lot!

"But then I feel that I *shouldn't* like it," Colin adds. The problem is that, in a sense, Colin has benefited from his brother's death. The closer relationship he now has with his parents is possible because Jason is no longer alive. And this makes Colin feel guilty.

Like many bereaved adolescents, the impact of losing their brothers didn't really hit Colin or Julie at first. Since neither felt a lot of pain in the beginning, they thought this meant they were bad people or didn't really care. "I don't know why, but I didn't cry very much," Colin says. "It makes you feel bad, like you didn't really love him or something," he adds painfully.

Julie's feelings were very similar. "I thought there was something wrong with me when my brother first died—that I wasn't feeling the pain right away," she recalls. "I felt guilty and I was mad at myself. I didn't understand why. Was I a bad sister or something?"

For both these young people, it's been a real relief to learn that not feeling much at first is a common experience, and that it doesn't mean they didn't care. "Well, some of the people in my group also didn't cry," Colin states. "So that made me feel like it wasn't just me. It took some guilt away."

The natural friction between brother and sister or parent and child can be a source of later guilt even when there was no way of knowing at the time that the other person might die. Abby wasn't always in the mood when her brother wanted his back scratched. Now, the times she refused bother her a lot. "I find myself saying to myself, 'I wish I hadn't been such a *jerk* about scratching his back! What was the *big deal*?' I know it sounds like such a stupid, idiot thing," she says, "but it's not." Not now that Ben's dead.

It's even worse when words said in anger come back to haunt you later. "I think what I really regret," Stephanie admits, "is that I used to say, 'I hate you! I wish you'd die!' One time I said that to her—I didn't know she was sick—and the look on her face! It was really quick but she looked so hurt!"

Angry statements like this are normal in the tumultuous relationships between teenagers and their parents and would have been forgotten if Stephanie's mother hadn't died. But knowing this isn't helping Stephanie much right now. "I regret ever saying that because it wasn't true!" she says with despair. "I always say dumb things when I'm mad. I wish I didn't feel so much guilt!" she adds. "I'm really hoping I'll get over it. I didn't even mean any of those things!"

As her mother's condition deteriorated, Stephanie faced other guilt-inducing situations. Like most teens who must cope with the fact that someone they love is dying a slow, painful death, Stephanie wanted to be with her mother as much as possible, to help her in any way she could. But she also needed a break from the physically revolting aspects of her mother's progressive cancer.

Adults also feel guilty when they find themselves repelled by a loved one's illness, but they are able to understand that their response is unavoidable and out of their control. But, like most adolescents in this situation, Stephanie expected more of herself. "I guess I was being selfish," she says, remembering the times when she couldn't put aside her own distress enough to focus completely on her mother.

The issue of "selfishness" comes up in other areas as well. Erica felt guilty because she still wanted to have a life of her own, even if her stepmother, Sharon, was in the hospital. "You know, that whole time she was in the hospital, I was being really selfish," she recalls. "I started going out with my boyfriend and we'd go dancing. And I'd still go to work. I was being *selfish*. I mean, I saw my aunts and my grandparents and everybody else—their lives *stopped* for her because she was sick. And mine didn't."

Erica's situation was complicated by her fury that her stepmother's alcoholism, which had already caused Erica so much pain, now resulted in Sharon's being the center of everyone else's concern and attention. Still, if she had known how guilty she would feel later, Erica thinks she might have done things differently. "I wish I'd known what the experience was going to feel like, how it was going to affect me," she acknowledges. "I would have thought more about it—about what was really happening."

Perhaps the worst problem in having a friend or family member who is terminally ill is not knowing what to wish for—whether you should pray that they live or that they die. As Jay says, "You'd say, 'God, put her to sleep now and don't let her suffer.' And if that happened, you'd say, 'God, why couldn't you just let her live some more?' It's hard. It's a double confusion." And a real breeding ground for guilt.

Julie's decision left her with a crippling sense of responsibility for her brother's death, a feeling that has only recently started to go away. "When he was getting really, really sick—the last two weeks—my mom asked everyone to pray that he'd die so that he wouldn't be in pain anymore," Julie says. "And I used to get mad at her! I didn't want to pray for him to die. I wanted him to get better! So, every night when she asked us to pray that he would die, I would pray that he *wouldn't* die!"

But Denis just got sicker and sicker. "Sometimes, if he was in a lot of pain—this would scare everybody—he'd yell out, 'I want to die!' And you knew he wanted to get it over with, you could tell.

"What happened that evening," Julie continues painfully, "was he had problems breathing and they had to bring the oxygen in. And I saw him struggling, you know. And then I said, 'Why should he go on like this, if there's no way he can get better? And he *isn't!*'

"I didn't want him to go on in that pain," she explains. "So, that night, I remember lying in bed and I prayed that he would die. I finally said to myself that he wouldn't have any pain anymore. And he died that night," she adds softly.

"For a long time afterward, I thought it was my fault," Julie admits. "A part of me felt that I was holding on by praying that he wouldn't die—and that I cut loose."

In a strange way, Elaine felt almost guilty that she didn't die or, more accurately, that she was still alive. She and Mandy had been so close that Elaine felt her mere presence was a painful reminder to Mandy's parents that their own daughter was gone. "It was painful to see Mandy's parents. I think also because it was painful for them," she recalls.

The sense that seeing her was difficult for Mandy's parents lasted well into Elaine's college years. Occasionally, Elaine would run into Mandy's mother, who would ask about her life. "I would tell her I was going to college, or whatever. And it would be a funny feeling," Elaine admits, "because I would feel that she was thinking, 'Oh, I wonder if Mandy would have been in college there.' So it was awkward."

Bereaved adolescents can also feel guilty about their inability to help others cope with the death. In spite of his conscious effort to ward off all emotions, Gary is very attuned to his mother's emotional pain. He wants desperately to be supportive to her, but he doesn't know how. "Every time I looked at her, I felt guilty," he says. "I felt so sorry for her and I just didn't know what to do."

Vicky would like to be able to talk about her mother, but she feels guilty even mentioning her. Although talking about the person who died is a healthy way of dealing with loss, Vicky's father finds it hurts too much to think about his wife. And Vicky doesn't want to cause him any more pain.

"I live with my father," she explains, "and he's very closed off about it. He doesn't like talking about it and he tries to wipe out every memory of my mother ever living." As a result, Vicky has come to feel that mentioning her mother to anyone is almost taboo. "I always feel guilty bringing up her name, like I shouldn't say it," she adds.

Finally, the death of a parent means that the remaining parent must fill the role of both mother and father. When doing this seems to impose a heavy burden on the parent, children may feel they are responsible. After her mother's death, Vicky's father devoted himself to raising her, neglecting his own social life. When she began dating, the thought of her father sitting home alone made her feel terrible. "I felt so guilty because I would go out and I said, 'This man pulled himself out of the social scene to stay home with me when I was younger, and now here he is suffering because of that. He doesn't have any friends, he hasn't met anybody new—maybe there was that someone special out there that he could have met, but he didn't because of me.' And I felt really guilty, as if I ruined his life."

Fortunately, Vicky feels differently now. She has begun to see that her father chose to do what he did of his own free will. And there's been another development that's made things a lot easier. "Just recently," Vicky adds, "he started dating this woman. And I love the fact that they are going out!"

9 / Feeling Crazy/Feeling Suicidal

*I thought I was crazy. One minute, I'd really
want her to be here! And then I'd think, "I
hate her! I hate her! I can't believe she did
this to me!" I thought I was becoming
schizophrenic.*—MEGAN

*When you go through something like the death
of someone you love, part of you leaves you and
there's not enough of you inside to be yourself.
Something else comes inside of you, something
different. And you feel like doing evil things, things
that are not normal for you.*—PAM

FOR SOME grieving teenagers, the period after the
numbness wears off can be unbearably difficult. Buf-
feted by painful and conflicting emotions, they feel
totally overwhelmed. Sometimes, their emotions, as
well as their own behavior, seem so out of control
that it actually feels as if they are going crazy. Watching themselves become people they don't even recognize, they increasingly lose hope that they'll ever be
able to handle living. When this happens, some bereaved adolescents consider killing themselves.

Although many bereaved people have suicidal wishes, these thoughts are usually infrequent and short-lived. When thoughts of suicide occur more often, however, it's important for the person to talk about them and to get help. At one point, both Megan and Pam experienced recurring suicidal feelings. Fortunately, they managed to find ways out of what seemed at the time to be impossible situations. For both, learning that they were not alone, that other bereaved teenagers felt the way they did, was a critical part of being able to get their lives back together again.

In spite of the fact that she loved her mother desperately, for the first year after her death, Megan felt very little. Then, at the beginning of the second year, the pain hit with full force. "The numbing was over and it was all right there!" she recalls. "The whole thing was right there and it was too big and too overwhelming to do anything. I didn't know how to deal with it! It was just *amazing* pain."

The shock of her mother's death would fade, only to return again and again. "A couple of times a week it would hit. I'd think, 'Oh, no! My mother's dead! There's no way! No!' It just kept coming and coming."

Complicating her ability to deal with this pain were the conflicting emotions she felt towards her mother. "I would get really angry!" she says. "I had a picture of her and I would come home and throw it against the wall. That sounds crazy, but I'd get so furious! I wouldn't want anything around the house that would remind me of her."

At other times, all she wanted was to touch her mother's clothes. "We didn't clean out her closet and I used to go in there and I would just sit and look at her clothes. I would go through them and I would read things she had written. I just wanted to be with her so badly," she remembers painfully.

These dramatic mood swings terrified her. "I was really scared!" Megan says. "I thought, 'I can't believe this! Am I normal? Am I going to be crazy? What's going to happen?'"

Not surprisingly, Megan had difficulty focusing on schoolwork and, as her grades plummeted, she began to despair of ever getting into college.

"Everything just went downhill," she recalls. "I did really badly in school. My grades dropped dramatically." Worse, no one seemed to notice that she was in trouble. "None of my teachers ever mentioned anything to me. No one cared!" she says.

As things continued to crumble around her, Megan began to give up. "I thought, 'I can't deal with it.' It just kept coming and coming. And I just wanted to turn off the switch. I wanted it to totally end!"

It would also be a way to join her mother. "I really wanted to be with my mother, you know," Megan recalls. "And I thought, 'That's the only way.' It was just too hard to handle and I was doing it all by myself and I couldn't."

Somehow, Megan grabbed hold of her situation and decided to try a different approach. "I took the initiative," she says. "I thought, 'I can't do this by myself. There's no way.'" So Megan began to confide in her father, who provided a lot of understanding and support. She also went to a counselor at school who was able to convince her that she wasn't finished academically, that she still had a future—both in school and out.

Perhaps most important, however, was learning that she wasn't crazy after all and that other kids had gone through what she was experiencing and had survived. A social worker introduced her to a boy at school who had also lost his mother, and they became good friends. "He's been a big help," Megan says. "He told me, 'I understand exactly what you're going through. It's fine. Don't think that you're crazy. Just let the feelings flow, just deal with them and accept them.' It was hard to," Megan adds, "but I did it."

She also joined a bereavement group for teenagers. Because Megan is uncomfortable talking in front of a lot of people, she doesn't say much there. But she gets a lot out of listening. "I would go to the group and just listen and then I would go home and cry," Megan says. "What helped was to know that they were going through the same thing."

Even better, the kids she met there were not just struggling along, they were really doing OK. It's been good for Megan to see others who've had more experience, like one girl whose mother died four years ago. "I look at her," Megan says. "And she's still here, she's still going through life, she's normal, she's getting through it."

Megan has begun to feel she's getting through it too. "I can't say it's over," she comments. "But I feel I've really started to deal with my mother's death and accept it. My life's starting back up again," Megan adds, smiling.

It's still hard, though. "Sometimes, I want to go to the teacher and say, 'Listen, I can't deal with this class right now.' But then I think, 'But I really want to be normal, I really want to be like the rest of the kids, so I'm just going to stand it.' And I go on to my next class."

Pam's mother knew Pam was in serious trouble, she just didn't know what to do about it. Pam was seeing a counselor, but that didn't seem to be helping much. So her mother just tried not to do anything that would rock the boat.

"She was afraid to say no to me," Pam remembers. "I mean, it would be three o'clock in the morning and I would come in and say, 'Can I borrow your car for a ride?' And she would say yes, when normally she'd say, 'What are you talking about? It's three in the morning!' "

Pam was so absorbed in her own pain that she didn't notice that either she or her mother was behaving unusually. Finally, things got pretty extreme. "She used to not like me to stay out after one in the morning," Pam says. "And I wasn't coming in until four o'clock. I'd get upset and I'd be with my friends and I just couldn't deal with coming home at the time, but she never said anything because she didn't want me to get upset."

Pam's mother was terribly worried by Pam's behavior. But Pam didn't know what to do with herself either. She was so miserable without Brian she could barely breathe. She was also very, very angry. "I would sit there and say, 'What did I do to deserve this?' Our relationship was so perfect, so golden. I felt like I was being punished!"

In her unhappiness, she began to take her pain out on others. "It's just that you feel so much," Pam explains. "And you think, 'Forget this! I'm not going to be the only one! I'm going to do things to other people.'

"I started to lead guys on and make them think I liked them." After letting them get close to her, Pam would drop them. "And then I felt, 'Ha! Ha! You're hurt!' I was purposefully hurting people," she admits. "And I didn't really know what I was doing."

Her friends became angry with her and confronted her with her behavior. When she realized what she was doing, Pam got very upset. "I felt horrible," she remembers. "I thought I was an evil person. This wasn't the kind of person I wanted to be. I thought, 'Get me out of here! I can't be around these people, I can't do these things to people!' "

The solution seemed obvious. "I thought, 'Forget it! I've got to be with Brian! I can't make it without Brian. I wasn't like this when I was with Brian, so the only thing for me is to be with him!' "

The thing that stopped her was the thought of inflicting further pain on her parents and Brian's family. Pam just couldn't bear to do that to them. Then both her mother and Brian's mom suggested that she attend a bereavement group for adolescents. "The only reason I went," Pam says, "was because my mom and Brian's mom were in tears saying, 'Please try it!' The only reason I tried it was for them, not for myself." To her surprise, the group turned out to be a lifesaver.

It really helped to know that she wasn't the only one, that she hadn't been somehow singled out for all this pain. "You know," Pam says, describing her feelings when she first entered the group, "*I* was the one that was hurting. *Nobody* hurt as much as me! But you realize through group," she continues, "that it's normal to feel that way, that everyone does.

"But you're not the only one. You know, it's 'Why me?' all the time. But then you realize, it's not 'Why me?' It's 'Why all these people too?' It's not something I did wrong," she adds, "or he did wrong, or she did wrong. It's just something that happened." And knowing this has made a big difference.

Others haven't been as lucky as Megan and Pam. Two of Brian's friends have been on the thin edge since Brian died. "His best friend ended up on drugs and had to go into rehab," Pam says. "And another—first he got rid of his motorcycle. Then he went out and got a new one and he stopped wearing his helmet." Whether these boys are consciously trying to kill themselves or not, death could easily be the end result of their behavior.

Sadly, some bereaved adolescents do more than think about suicide. Adam's brother's best friend was a real source of support for Adam after his brother died. A year later, however, he shot himself. No one really knows why he did what he did. There were other things going wrong in his life besides the loss of Adam's brother. But the death of a close friend or a family member can sometimes be more than a teenager can handle without help.

Fortunately, there are many sources of help to which bereaved adolescents can turn if they feel overwhelmed or suicidal. As Megan discovered, confiding in a parent can be a good place to start. Not only can parents offer support themselves but, as in Pam's case, they may assist in locating professional help.

Sometimes, however, parents may be too involved in their own grief to respond appropriately to a teenager's request for help. In other instances, the teenager may find it too difficult to discuss frightening suicidal thoughts with parents. When this happens, bereaved adolescents should turn to other adults in their community who can help. Relatives, school counselors, mental health professionals, clergy, and the parents of friends are all people who care and will listen.

Finally, many of the bereaved teenagers interviewed for this book found professional help of one kind or another to be useful, even if they weren't feeling suicidal. Of all the forms of counseling available, the most popular were bereavement groups, especially those designed for teenagers. Local mental health clinics, hospital social service departments, and churches or synagogues can help bereaved people find one of these groups in their community.

10 / When You Weren't Wild About Them in the First Place

But when he died, I wished that he didn't die! I don't know why I felt that way because I never really liked him.—MARIE

Maybe this dream will mean something: I came into the house and they were standing there, my dad and Sharon. I knew that she was dead and she had come back to life. And I said, "Get out of here! We're all getting over you now. I don't want you here!" And my dad said, "It's OK, Erica. She's just here for a little bit. She's going to leave again." And I was yelling, "No!" I was afraid she was going to come back and ruin us again. When we're all making so much progress.—ERICA

FAMILY members don't always like each other. They may not even love each other very much. Sometimes, it's difficult to know what the feelings are. Not surprisingly, it's hard to understand how you feel when someone dies if you were never really sure what you felt about them when they were alive. For Marie, Lynette, and Erica, this has been a real problem.

Marie and Lynette's father left them to come to the United States when Marie was four and Lynette almost two. Ten years later, their mother brought the family here to rejoin him. By then, the girls' father was a stranger to them. When he died three years later, Marie and Lynette still barely knew him.

"He'd work at night, come home during the day. He'd be sleeping, I'd be in school," Marie says. "When he got up to go to work, I'd be sleeping. So I never got to see him much."

When they did get to see him, the girls didn't care much for what they saw. A stern man, he had a hard way about him that didn't encourage closeness. "I was scared," Lynette recalls. "Well, not really scared, but the way he looked sometimes, I didn't want to get close to him."

Worse, he was physically abusive at times. "He *hit* on his kids. And I didn't like that!" Marie says emphatically.

So, it came as a shock to both girls when they found themselves grieving after his death. "I thought it was something I wouldn't really care about," Lynette says with surprise. "But it hurts me that he's not alive anymore." In order to deal with this unexpected pain, she reminds herself that they didn't get along. "If you remember when he was mean to you," she says, "then you don't miss him so much."

Since her father died, Marie has begun to remember the happier times she shared with him as a very young child—memories she had forgotten. "Why these things come back to me now, I don't know," she says. "I really didn't like this man very well."

Marie struggles to make sense of her feelings. "I mean, if you really didn't like the person, you probably wouldn't even care," she concludes. "But as a family, even though you didn't like the person, you would still feel the pain. You would still feel sorry."

Erica had good reason to be angry at her stepmother. Sharon had been an alcoholic for years. She was a quiet, hard-working, successful woman, but an alcoholic nevertheless. This was particularly disappointing to Erica, who had hoped her father's home would be a refuge from the chaos she'd experienced living with her mother.

But when she moved in with her father and Sharon, she could tell something was very wrong. Erica had had plenty of practice spotting this sort of thing before—with her mother and stepfather. She even tried to do something about the problem, but there wasn't much she could accomplish by herself. "When I first lived with them, when I was in junior high, I told my grandparents and my family, 'They drink too much! I'm sorry, but they *drink too much*!' But no one listened to me," Erica recalls.

Finally, Erica moved back with her mother, where the situation had improved. But when she started college in the city where her father lived, she returned to his house. Things had gotten worse in her absence.

"And then when I moved back, Sharon had hepatitis. She went to the doctor, and I knew she was drinking all this time. I'd come home and she'd be passed out on the couch," Erica says. "You could smell the stuff on her, and you'd find hidden glasses in the kitchen and behind the bed. My dad and I knew what was going on but we never said anything to anybody," she adds. They never said anything about it to each other either.

It was a pretty lonely life. "He'd be in the living room, she would be in the bedroom, I would be in my bedroom, and none of us were talking or communicating. I was really unhappy!" Erica remembers. "I knew she drank too much, I knew my dad drank too much. Instead of doing anything, I just moved out."

A month later, Sharon was in the hospital, dying. "I went to visit her in the hospital. We weren't really close. I couldn't say a lot to her," Erica says.

It wasn't just that they weren't close. Erica was furious at Sharon. "She was causing *us* pain by what she had done! And that made me mad! In fact," Erica admits, "it's almost like I *wanted* her to die. This is very bad to say, but I wanted her to go because I knew I'd be closer to my dad."

Feeling the way she did, it was hard for Erica to visit Sharon. "It was just very uncomfortable for me, because I couldn't really express, you know, 'I want you to get better and stuff.'" Erica didn't go back to the hospital again until right before Sharon died.

In spite of all this, Erica cared about Sharon and it hurt when she died. "It wasn't like I had a close, close relationship with her," Erica says. That would have been hard, as Sharon was difficult to get close to. "She could be really cold when she wanted to," explains Erica. "She never really opened up to anybody."

But Sharon hadn't always been an alcoholic, and when Erica was a child her stepmother had tried to be good to her. "We were close, but then we weren't," Erica says. "I know I loved her, because she did a whole lot for me. But, you know, I think she always wanted kids and we never really filled the void for her. It was kind of hard, I think, for her," she adds sadly.

Like Marie and Lynette, Erica feels conflicting emotions about her stepmother's death. "She was a big part of my life," Erica says. "But I'm not really sure what I felt for her. Then, all of a sudden, she was in a coma and then she was gone. I didn't know how to react. Even now, I still don't really know how I'm feeling."

It may take Erica—and Marie and Lynette—a while to figure this out.

11 / Friends

I don't understand them! I didn't tell them, but they heard about it and they acted like nothing happened!—LYNETTE

My closest friend, Wendy, helped me a lot. Just going out with me, talking with me.—BRENDA

As ADOLESCENTS become more independent of their families, they turn more to friends for emotional support. Under the best of circumstances, however, relationships with friends are not problem free. The death of a family member or close friend places added pressures on a bereaved teenager's friendships, sometimes straining them to a breaking point. This is particularly hard when the teenager's parents, because of their own grief, are emotionally unavailable to provide needed support.

Both Lynette and Marie were bitterly disappointed by the reaction of friends to their father's death. "Well, I just said, 'What kind of friends are they?' I mean, my father dying and they were acting like . . . nothing!" Lynette exclaims.

Yet Lynette doesn't seem to be exactly sure how they should act. True, she doesn't want to be reminded of her father's death, since this intensifies the pain. She suspects that her friends know this and that this may be one reason they don't approach her. "I don't know," she says, when asked why she thinks they don't say much about it. "I guess because they didn't want me to think about it or something.

"But even if they didn't say anything, they didn't even show it!" Lynette adds angrily. Just how they should show it isn't clear either. "They should kind of feel sorry for my feelings," she says, haltingly.

If Lynette's friends are having difficulty responding to her father's death, it's not unusual. Many people feel uncomfortable in this situation and, fearing they will say the wrong thing, they avoid saying anything at all. In Lynette's case, it seems likely that her friends may also have some trouble figuring out how she wants them to respond.

Her sister Marie is unhappy with friends for different reasons. They initially responded, but not in the way she wanted. "Of course, they said how sorry they were and things like that," she says, "but that bothered me because I didn't want to hear it. Telling me that they're sorry just makes me feel sad."

Yet Marie was hurt and furious when some schoolmates didn't express sorrow at her father's death. "If a friend of yours knows and she didn't come to you and say how sorry she was, you would feel that the person didn't care! But still, when they come and say it to you, you feel, 'Why are you telling me that? It doesn't help!' I mean, the person is already dead."

Eight months have passed and Marie seems to want to talk more about her feelings than she did at first. But her friends, perhaps effectively silenced by Marie's earlier reaction, don't give her an opening. "Friends, people I know, don't talk about it too much. I mean, have they forgotten already?" she asks. "Nobody ever asks me, 'How are you doing?' Nobody. Maybe they're just afraid to mention it because they know I didn't like it when they came to me and said how sorry they were. I think that's why they don't." Marie's needs have changed over time, but she has trouble letting friends know that.

Like Lynette and Marie, Kristen was also very disappointed in the lack of support offered by friends. "I had a lot of problems with my friends. They weren't great friends," she says.

Kristen's situation was complicated by additional factors. Since her parents were divorced and she lives with her mother, her friends apparently didn't realize how connected she felt to her father. Perhaps more important, Kristen's way of grieving may have resulted in miscommunication.

"At the time," Kristen recalls, "I expected my friends to do just what I thought they should do—be nice to me. If they have a problem, I listen. So I expected that *they* should listen to *me*."

A reasonable expectation, but Kristen doesn't seem to have said much—or showed much either. "I don't cry in front of people. I don't even cry in front of my mom," she says. "So they told me that they didn't know it meant so much to me because I didn't demonstrate that it meant anything to me."

Not only did her friends fail to see how much her father's death upset her, but they had difficulty understanding her behavior in general. "I didn't want to do things. I wanted to be left alone. And they didn't get that," Kristen continues.

"I mean, I walked into a classroom one day and there were all my friends gathered together saying, 'She's so weird! Why is she acting this way? What's the big deal? So her father died—she wasn't that close to him anyway.' So I walked out."

When the initial numbness of the first year lifted and Kristen began to feel her loss even more intensely, her friends were totally befuddled. "That made it harder, because my friends couldn't understand it the first time," Kristen recalls. "And they really couldn't understand it a *year later*! I mean, they thought, 'Finally it's over.' And then a year later and, 'What, again?' I imagine that was pretty weird."

Weird or not, it was the last straw. Kristen dropped the circle of friends she had relied on for years and began to seek out people she felt would be more responsive. It wasn't easy. "When you've been in the same school since the third grade, it's really hard to make friends with people you've known that long," Kristen explains, "because it's obvious you haven't tried to be friends with them before."

The dissatisfaction expressed by Lynette, Marie, and Kristen seems to be a common feeling. Like them, Erica feels somehow let down by friends, particularly her boyfriend. On some level, she's aware that the problem may be at least partly her fault. But that doesn't stop it from hurting, or stop her from expecting others to know what to do anyway.

"Most of my friends say they're really sorry and we drop it at that. For instance, with my boyfriend, I don't know what to say. I don't know how to open up because I don't know what I'm feeling now," Erica says. "I think my boyfriend just doesn't know what to do. He's not the kind of person who knows exactly what to say. I hold that against him sometimes."

Often, what bereaved teenagers really want from their friends may be impossible for anyone to give— a word or an action that makes the pain go away. Some, like Vicky, come to realize this. "I guess my guidelines were set up of the exact person that I wanted, but I didn't even know what that was, so I could never find the right person to talk to," she says. "I wanted someone who made me comfortable, and I don't know how that could have been."

But there are many times when bereaved adolescents turn to friends and are able to find the solace they need. The fact that many teens are able to be there for a grief-stricken friend is a tribute to the strength of adolescent friendships and to the ability of teenagers to reach out to each other. Both Marie and Erica managed to find one friend who provided the support they needed, and Kristen has made new friends with whom she feels more comfortable.

Others were fortunate enough to have friends that were helpful from the beginning. "I have really affectionate friends," Jay says proudly. "They're really nice and they help me through a lot of stuff. Tom is my best friend. Whenever I need to talk to someone, he'll just sit there and listen to me."

Jay is lucky. As a boy, he feels a lot of pressure not to cry. But his friends understand. "With me, a lot of people know what's happened to me. So they won't come out and say, 'You're a wimp!'"

Brenda's closest friend was almost as upset by her brother's death as she was. Together, they consoled each other. "My friends helped me a lot," Brenda remembers, "especially Wendy. We had been best friends since we were nine years old. She always had a crush on Larry, so she was very, very hurt. We'd just sit down and talk about him."

In some cases, friends did more than just respond. Occasionally, they were able to anticipate what a bereaved person needed—even when that person, like Abby, was too dazed to know herself. Abby had received the news of her brother's death in an especially traumatic way. She was awakened in the middle of the night by people screaming that Ben had died. The experience left her afraid to go to sleep in her room.

"One girl would come here in the afternoon and she'd stay with me all evening," Abby remembers. "And I'd go to bed at ten or eleven and she'd put me to bed and would stay with me till I was asleep, which was like real, loving friendship!"

Pam doesn't think she would have survived after Brian's death if it hadn't been for their friends. "There was a group of about twenty of us," she says. "It helped for all of us to stick so close together. I don't think I would have gotten along without them and then again, I don't think they would have gotten along without me or any of the other kids, for that matter."

Although initially they were able to be a strong source of support for each other, eventually Brian's death appears to have been too much for the group to handle. "None of us are together anymore," Pam says. "It surprised me a lot. I never expected any of us to drift, but I'm not close to any of those people anymore."

There seem to have been a number of reasons for this, one of them being a fear of risking further loss. "I don't know," Pam muses, "maybe we were all afraid to lose each other."

Then, too, everyone seemed to change after Brian died, Pam included. "My old crowd seems stupid to me now," Pam admits. A couple of the guys got into some really self-destructive behavior. And Pam didn't like where the others were headed either. "All they wanted to do was just hang out and do nothing. It seemed that they were all going nowhere, they were all doing nothing, they were all living for themselves."

As the one closest to Brian, Pam continued to grieve well after the others were getting over their sorrow, and this difference between them made it hard for both Pam and her friends. "And then everybody got kind of sick of me always talking about it," she says.

Finally, Pam was jealous—a problem that often springs up between bereaved teenagers and their friends. "One couple didn't want to hang out with us anymore because they felt bad because they were so happy and I had to lose Brian. And it's true!" Pam admits angrily. "That did bother me. I hated seeing them together! They knew it and I think that was one of the reasons they stayed away."

Although there's no question that friends can and frequently do provide the support a bereaved adolescent needs, sometimes the best support is a teenager who's experienced a similar loss. Although it's possible to find another bereaved individual to talk to, often the best place is a bereavement group. Here, no one is surprised or annoyed that the person is still struggling with the death two, three, or four years later. The jealousy that can hamper relationships is gone when everyone experiences the deprivation. And emotions that seem too strange, too confusing, or too bad to talk about suddenly become acceptable when others are feeling them too.

Many young people who have had access to groups in which they can share their feelings with others who understand, first-hand, what they're talking about have found it especially helpful. Jay has belonged to two such groups. First he attended a group for siblings of cancer patients. Now he's part of a group in his town for teenagers who have lost a close friend or family member.

Jay has gotten so much out of these experiences that when he heard Colin had lost a brother, he reached out and brought him to a meeting. Colin is very grateful that he did. "It was a good surprise!" Colin says. "I didn't even know that he knew me."

Although it's been three years since his brother died, Colin hadn't really been able to talk about his feelings. As he says, "I'd been kind of keeping them bottled up inside." Now, with peers, he's learning that the emotions that were making him feel so guilty aren't unusual after all. And knowing that makes a big difference.

Finally, friends don't necessarily have to be human beings. Although Gary unexpectedly found himself pouring out his heart to a sympathetic guy at school, he doesn't have many people he's comfortable opening up to. That's why his pets have been such a help. "The first months, every time I'd start to feel lonely or sad, a dog would come in and push its nose in my face, or a cat would jump on top of me," he recalls. "It was good just to have a warm body coming up to you that would just accept you."

Part Four
Putting the Family Back Together Again

THE DEATH of a parent or a sibling creates special problems for surviving family members. In addition to dealing with the pain of losing someone they loved, bereaved family members must struggle to put their shattered family back together again. To do this, they must reach out to each other and establish new relationships that can bridge the gap in the family structure. For people whose emotional resources have been depleted by grief, this can be very difficult indeed.

Bereaved adolescents face extra complications in developing these new relationships. Because the death of a parent or sibling badly shakes a young person's sense of security, it usually intensifies his or her emotional dependence on the remaining family members. Unfortunately, this increased involvement, especially when directed toward parents, runs counter to the normal process of separating from the family that is characteristic of adolescence.

Moreover, bereaved parents have needs too, some of which may interfere with a teenager's natural attempts to become more independent. On the one hand, parents may become over-protective; on the other, they may lean too heavily on teenage children for support previously provided by a deceased spouse.

Bereaved teenagers, therefore, are caught between two conflicting pressures. Somehow, they must reestablish and strengthen their ties to family members while at the same time beginning to break away from them. Needless to say, this isn't easy.

Because of their strong emotional connections with family, holidays are particularly rough times for bereaved families trying to heal themselves. Well after much of the pain has receded and the family is back on an even keel, these days can be sorrowful reminders that someone special is missing.

12 / Healing the Wound
After the Death
of a Sibling

I figured, well, whatever he would have done [to help their parents], I should do for both of us.—ADAM

We [her remaining brother and herself] had to look at each other and say, "Hey, it's you and me, kid!"—ABBY

COMPARED to the death of a parent, the impact on a family of losing one of the children is often underestimated. But the pain, although different, is just as intense. For parents, the death of a child is a special trauma that can undermine even a good marriage. For the remaining children, the death means the loss of a unique support and friendship that are irreplaceable. Thus, the loss of a sibling creates a deep wound, one that the family must work hard to heal.

Although she has a little sister, Julie's younger brother Denis was the one closest in age to her. When he died, it left a hole in her life. "I didn't have that sibling close to me—that we could do things together, the same things," she explains. "You know, like talk about our parents behind their backs together."

Affectionate and close-knit people, her family weathered Denis's death fairly well. But there was still an empty space, something missing where Denis used to be. Then, two years ago, her parents adopted a baby boy. Julie makes it clear that this was not an attempt to replace her brother. "There's no way that he could replace Denis," she states emphatically. "That *anyone* could! That's not what we wanted.

"We wanted the opposite," she adds. "We wanted just some happiness to fill the emptiness. A new person to love, I guess."

Was it a good idea? "He's the best thing!" Julie says, smiling. "He really helped everybody. He kind of brought more happiness back."

It's changed things, of course. Not so much for Julie as for her little sister, who had to relinquish her place as the youngest in the family. "At first, she was jealous of losing all the attention," Julie says. "But now she's happy because she's the older sister and she can take care of him. He looks up to her and she likes that!"

By sharing their love with a new person, Julie's family has been able to strengthen their ties to one another. Careful not to adopt for the wrong reasons, they used their ability to reach out to successfully rebuild their family.

Brenda wasn't so lucky. When the older brother she idolized was suddenly killed, her family had trouble reaching out to each other. "I think everyone kind of pulled apart," she recalls. "Everyone went into their own little thing and didn't talk about it.

"I've never talked about Larry's death to my sister or my two brothers, really," she adds, with regret. "It seems no one wants to talk about him that much. My one brother, Ed, always talks about how he wishes he'd been closer to him, but that's it."

Why did Brenda's family have difficulty helping each other? It's hard to say. "Some parents ignore their kids," Brenda comments. "They feel so bad themselves, they don't realize that the siblings lost someone too."

Yet Brenda's mother, at least, seems to have wanted very much to respond to Brenda, to reach out to family members. "She never really locked me out," Brenda remembers, "because she tried to talk, to read about it. She went to groups about parents who've lost children, just to make sure that she treated her other children the proper way."

When asked what she thinks is important for bereaved families, Brenda answers, "I guess for the whole family to get close, to try to be close and not pull apart so much—families do have a tendency to let their own feelings just stay inside themselves and not really talk as a family about what happened. But they need to talk about it and not keep it inside." Sadly, however much Brenda's family may have wanted to do this, they didn't quite seem to know how.

Since his older sister's death, there have been many changes in Jay's relationship with his family. On the positive side, he's become much closer to his younger brother. "Before my sister died, we weren't really friends," he says. "But after, we had to cope with it and everything. Now my brother and I have gotten to be each other's best friend. We do everything together."

But there have been other changes in his family that Jay hasn't liked. His sister's death left his mother as the only female in the family, and Jay feels badly that she has no one of her own sex to talk to, to share with.

Also, after losing his sister, Jay's mother has become overprotective of him, curtailing activities that he was allowed to do when he was younger. "She won't let me ride my bike on the main road, which I used to do all the time," he complains. "And I used to go fishing alone and now she won't let me. She says, 'No, you might fall down and hit your head.'"

But perhaps the most difficult change for Jay to adjust to is that, with the death of his sister, he became the oldest child in the family, a position he doesn't like! Bringing home poor reports from school, for example, is much harder as the oldest sibling. "The way it used to be," he explains, "if my sister had done something before, then she would have broken the ice for me. And my parents wouldn't really mind as much, you know?"

Now that role has fallen to him. "But now I'm the oldest, and I have to break the ice for my brother," he says. "Like I'll be the first one to ask for a car, and later it won't be so hard for him."

It's more than just losing someone who smoothed the way for him, however. Jay also lost a person who could guide him and advise him—an older sibling who had more experience. He misses that a lot!

"If you've got problems in the eighth grade, like I do sometimes now, she'd always be there because she'd have gone through eighth grade," he says. "But now I can't talk to anybody but my guidance counselor. I can't talk to my little brother. It's funny because you don't know who to talk to when you're the oldest."

Things have changed in Adam's family too, but the differences are more subtle. Since his older brother's death, Adam has become more sensitive toward his parents. He's careful to come home from college for the holidays, for example, not just because he wants to but because he feels his parents need him there. "I think I come back for my mom," he says. "It's a holiday and even if we're not religious, we're thinking about family kinds of things."

And, although he seems to feel a little awkward about it, Adam tries hard to be supportive to both his parents. "Especially when they're upset," he says. "Not that there's much you can do, but you can just be there for them. I just let them cry on my shoulder."

Abby was shattered when Ben, her older brother, was killed in a car accident. But as painful as it was, Abby and her family managed to come out of the experience a closer unit, the connections between each of them stronger than before. As Abby puts it, "All four of us sort of interlocked. Either you get much closer or you go off on your own and you lose each other. And that's the *worst!*"

Abby had always been close to her mother, but it had clearly been a parent–child relationship in which she relied on her mother for support. With her brother's death, that changed somewhat. Her mother was in too much pain herself to be anyone else's source of strength. "There were times when I had to cry and she had to be strong for me. And she was," Abby recalls. "And then there were times when the roles were reversed—when I had to be strong for her and she had to cry."

Abby became closer to her oldest brother, Ron, after Ben died. But it was her father and his relationship with the rest of the family that changed the most. "I think my father experienced the most painful loss in his life," Abby says. "He felt Ben was the only one who accepted him unconditionally in the sense that, 'Whatever my dad does, it's the greatest!' Ron and I would question him more than Ben did."

As a result, there was a barrier between Ron and Abby and their father. "It was painful to me because I loved my father, but we were never really close. I didn't feel I knew him as a person and that always upset me," Abby recalls.

But when Ben died, Abby's father reached out to his family. "I think he realized," she explains, " 'If I don't get close to my kids now while I'm alive and while I have them, I'm never going to be close with them.'

"And he really opened up!" Abby says, smiling. "He's changed and he's let us get to know him more. And I began to accept him more because he showed more of his shortcomings. We got a lot closer." Like the other positive changes in Abby's family, this took a concentrated effort on everyone's part.

13 / Rebuilding the Family After the Death of a Parent

Our counselor said it the best: Your mother was the core of your apple, and when she was taken out, the apple started to rot.—VICKY

One night I walked downstairs—I couldn't go to sleep. And there she was, lying in the living room crying. I just sat there and put my arms around her.—GARY

ALTHOUGH the death of a parent is hard for children of any age, it poses special difficulties for adolescents. Without a stable parental foundation to return to, the process of exploring adult possibilities and alternatives seems much riskier. As a result, teenagers who have lost a parent may find it harder to forge their own mature values and identities.

Intensifying the problem is the fact that parents, unlike siblings, fill roles and perform functions that are vital to the family's well-being. When a parent dies, someone in the family must step in and pick up the slack. Most often, the person who does this is the remaining parent. Frequently, however, the bereaved parent is too overwhelmed with grief to do this effectively and adolescent children may be pressured into filling the place of the absent adult. This pressure is strongest when the adolescent is the same sex as the parent who died. Needless to say, it's hard for a teenager to fill an adult's role in any situation.

In Kristen's case, the problems involved in restructuring her family were less obvious than those faced by teenagers in two-parent households. Kristen's parents had divorced when she was very young and her father had remarried. For most of her life, she's lived alone with her mother. Thus, while her father's death was upsetting to both her mother and herself, it didn't disrupt their life as a family.

His death raised some problems about her relationships with other people, however, particularly her stepmother. Kristen had never been crazy about her father's last wife, but she maintained contact with her for about a year and a half after he died—not because she wanted to but because it had been his wish. "My father had told me that when he died, he wanted me to be friends with her," she explains. "And she always called me, so I figured, 'Well, why not, I don't care. I'll just talk to her every once in a while.'"

But her stepmother evidently wanted closer contact and this made Kristen uncomfortable. "She started picking me up at school. She did that twice and I didn't like it. So, I don't talk to her anymore," she says.

Kristen was also unsure what effect her father's death would have on her relationship with her half-siblings from his other marriages. In this case, however, she feared that with her father gone they would no longer feel a connection to her. "I was very worried at the time that they wouldn't want to talk to me, because I'm not really their sister, I'm their half-sister," she recalls.

To her great relief, this didn't happen. "I was at my brother's house and his friend said, 'You're not really Rickie's sister, you're his half-sister.' And I didn't know what to say to that. But my brother said, 'She's my sister! She's not my half-sister, she's my sister.' And I was just ecstatic with this! The fact that he said that made me so happy!" Her other brother and sister clearly have similar feelings. Although they don't live in the area, they both keep in close touch with her.

In spite of her complicated family situation, Kristen has managed to hold onto the relationships that are important to her. Things are not going as well for Gary. Although he's the youngest of three siblings, when his father died, he became the man of the house—a role he feels completely unprepared for. "It's more responsibility, more pressure," he sighs, "just knowing that I'm the man of the house."

Gary obviously feels overwhelmed by the job. "Whatever happens," he says, "I'm responsible. If someone breaks into the house, I'm responsible. If the car gets into an accident, I feel it's my responsibility. When our dog got sick, I thought it was my responsibility. Just so much more stuff has been put on me. I don't know if I was really ready for it. I'd like to just go back," he says sadly, "but I can't."

In addition to seeing that things are taken care of around the house, there are other, more subtle pressures on Gary. He and his mother are the only ones living at home, and Gary knows that she leans on him for emotional support. In some ways, that's been all right. "We've gotten closer," he says. "We've gotten to know each other better. I feel like she's really talking more."

On the other hand, they haven't had much choice. "With just two people living in the house, it's hard not to get to know each other," he adds wryly. And when the other person needs someone, that someone is you. "It's also that you have no privacy," he adds. "When one person wants to talk, there's only one other person in the house to talk to."

Even away from the house, Gary finds he has less privacy. Since his father's death, his mother has become more concerned about his whereabouts. "Now she knows when I'm going out, who I'm going with, when I'll be back, what I'm doing," Gary says. He also feels a greater pressure to be home on time so his mother doesn't have to worry about him.

His father's death has affected his relationships with his older siblings as well. Until then, Gary didn't really know his sister. "I was always the little brother who got in the way of her dates," he says. Although she's away at college now, they've gotten much closer. "When this happened," Gary explains, "we just started talking. Every time that we saw each other, we sat down and started to talk."

It's a different story with his older brother, however. Gary feels that some of the responsibility he has had to shoulder should have been shared by his brother, John. But John split.

Gary is furious with him! "The way I see it," he says angrily, "he abandoned us. He left six months after Dad died, just left to go to California. He couldn't stay here and help out!"

Gary tries to understand the situation from his brother's point of view. John had angered their parents by dropping out of college to work as a courier. "So when my dad died," says Gary, "he must have felt guilty and just wanted to get away from everything that would remind him of that. So he stayed for as long as he could and then just left." But knowing this isn't much comfort to Gary.

Like Gary, Megan felt pressured to step into an adult role and, like him, she found it too much to handle. When her parents went to Germany for treatment of her mother's cancer, Megan was left at home with her two older brothers. "So we were all by ourselves, which was really hard," she recalls. "I became like the mother of the house. I cleaned and kind of tried to cook and stuff and it just didn't work! My brothers would never listen to me. I finally gave up," she adds. "It's a little too much to take over!"

Megan had always been extremely close to her mother. When she died, Megan had to learn to relate to her father, something that was very difficult at first. "It was a really hard time. I didn't know my dad at all," she says. "I had never really dealt with him before by myself." With her mother gone, Megan felt isolated in a family full of males. "Before, I had my mother on my side. Now I was alone with my dad and my brothers. It was really hard."

But Megan's father is a caring man and together the two of them were able to forge new bonds. "My dad, now he's kind of like my mom and my dad. We talk about things that I used to tell my mom. I mean, there are things that it's hard to talk about, but he's really supportive of me."

Erica's gotten much closer to her father too. But her situation is more complicated. Like some other children of divorced parents, Erica felt shut off from her father, unable to have the relationship with him that she wanted. She blamed her stepmother, Sharon, for her father's lack of interest in her.

"My dad was so caught up in what was going on with Sharon," Erica explains. "She was an alcoholic and he was drinking and they weren't happy. And so he was kind of shutting everyone else out." Frustrated and miserable with the situation, Erica left to live with other relatives.

When Sharon died, however, Erica moved back in with her father and eagerly stepped into the role that Sharon had filled. In some ways, this was exactly what she had wanted—to be the main person in her father's life. In other ways, it was creepy. "It was weird!" Erica remembers. "I was doing the shopping, using her pots and pans. I was even in her car. It was a terrible feeling."

Slowly, Erica became aware of the down side of being the focus of her father's life—his increasing dependence on her. "Sometimes I'd feel, 'What if I left? What would happen to him?'"

This was not what she'd bargained for. "I don't *like* this!" she thought. "I'm not his *wife*! I'm his daughter!" Fortunately, something happened that changed things. "Then my dad got a girl friend," Erica says. "And it eased up the pressure on me."

Since Sharon's death, Erica's father has really tried to open up to her. "Well, basically with my dad," she says with a smile, "we're just like a hundred percent closer! It's a totally different relationship because we're talking to each other now."

But Erica and her father are still struggling to achieve a healthy balance in relating to each other. For one thing, they're trying to define whether they're father and daughter, friends, or both. Since the foundation of their relationship was shaky to begin with, it's taking a lot of effort for them to put their family back together appropriately.

Then there's the matter of her father's girl friend. While Erica likes her and welcomes the fact that her presence takes a lot of the pressure off, she's still threatened by the fact that there's someone else her father cares about. "All my life," she says, "I wanted a father and he was never there. Now I have this relationship with my dad that I want. And I don't want anyone invading it!"

Jealousy over a surviving parent's new romantic interest is very common. But because she's always felt left out, the fact of her father's new relationship is scarier for Erica than for most bereaved teenagers.

Terry and Stephanie went through some really rough times at home after their mother died. For a while, it looked as if their father was going to be completely crushed by his grief. "My dad became a hermit," Stephanie recalls painfully. "He was really inside himself and wouldn't come out. He never cracked jokes, he never said anything. He never even looked at anyone else. He'd just come home every night and go in his bedroom.

"The house turned into a mess!" she adds. "Everything sort of went to pieces." Unfortunately, the series of housekeepers their father hired only made things worse.

"We had these live-in housekeepers and that was really bad," Terry says. "Some of them were just jerks and I didn't like any of them because I didn't like anyone trying to tell us what to do. They didn't even like us!"

A year passed and things still weren't much better. "I said something about my mom in the car," Stephanie remembers. "My dad had sunglasses on but I saw tears running down his cheeks. It was really hard on him. And I was *scared*! I didn't know what was going to happen to him."

Finally, their mom's best friend stepped in and introduced him to a woman who was much like their mother. The two started to date and the girls' father began to come out of his shell. "I think it's really nice," Stephanie says. "My dad's himself again!"

There are other pluses as well. "I can talk to her. She's really into girl things," Stephanie explains.

"And whenever she thinks my dad's being irrational about stuff, she sticks up for us."

Still, it hasn't all been smooth sailing. The first Christmas they spent together, their father lavished gifts on his girl friend. His daughters were hurt and angry. "I got jealous of Elisa," Stephanie admits. "She got *everything* that I got and even more! I was really upset!"

All in all, however, things are much better with Elisa around. Stephanie feels her father and Elisa will probably get married, and she'd like that. "I think it would be really nice to have someone I could call Mom again, to be really close to. It would be weird, *very* weird," she acknowledges. "But I think I could learn to deal with it."

While Terry and Stephanie's family came close to falling apart, Vicky's totally disintegrated. "We became very cold," she recalls. "No one wanted to depend on anybody because we were scared of losing that person. We could no longer function. We couldn't talk to each other on a one-to-one basis. There was no one to bridge the gap. And we just weren't used to reaching out and helping the other person. We had a lot of problems with that."

Some of the problems began before Vicky's mother died. "My father and brother have never gotten along," she says. With her mother's death, their relationship grew even more acrimonious. Finally, her father kicked her brother out of the house.

"My middle sister, Jill, took the burden of the family," Vicky continues. "She was twenty-seven years old and she was getting her life together. All of a sudden, her mother died and she dropped out of nursing school to stay home with a twelve-year-old—me—who someone had to raise.

"When I think about it now, I get sick because there was so much responsibility pushed on her—to take care of me, to cook for my father, to play housewife and mother," Vicky says. "She started to hate everyone in the family because they were putting so many demands on her. She kind of felt like she threw her life away and she was getting angry about that."

Eventually, the weight of these responsibilities proved too much. "She finally cracked under the pressure," Vicky recalls. "She couldn't keep up like that any longer." In real need of help, Jill left home and went into therapy.

At this point, there was no family left. "I was no longer allowed to see my brother," Vicky says. "My older sister threw herself into her work, my other sister had gone away—I didn't know where to—and my father was becoming so distant from me. The thing that was the saddest for me," she adds, "is that we always had such a close family and suddenly I was faced with the fact that I didn't only lose my mother, I lost my family."

But her family cared too much to give up without a fight. "Somehow, in my freshman year, our family grew back together again," Vicky says with relief. "I remember at my fifteenth birthday party, my sister Jill leaned over and hugged me. It was one of the first times that she'd shown any affection—that anyone in my family had shown affection in the last couple years."

Vicky sees her brother a lot now, but there are still problems. "My brother will never fully recover from my mother's death," she says. "He's so mad and hurt inside that his mother died that he kind of feels like the world owes him a living."

There's still a strain between her father and brother. "But besides that," Vicky says, "our family has become so incredibly strong. We spend every Sunday night together, we have dinner together, we're always together on the holidays.

"The initial loss, that really hurts a lot," Vicky comments, looking back. "But I personally believe that the most pain comes in the after-effects. I mean, I loved my mother and I missed her so much, but I wasn't caused the most pain from her death. I was caused the most pain by what happened to my family after. It took a really long time to become close again," she adds. But it was worth the struggle.

Whenever someone in a family dies, the relationships between remaining members are inevitably altered. Like a wagon that has lost a wheel, family members must learn to establish a new balance between them in order to avoid tipping over. These readjustments are difficult to make, but it is always easier if family members can pull together to help each other.

14 / Holidays and Anniversaries

I was so scared that she was going to die on my birthday! I thought, "Oh, she can't die on my birthday or I'll just go crazy!"—JAY

Basically, it's a hard day because all the memories come back. You think about what happened three years ago this day.—COLIN

THE ANNIVERSARY of a death can't help but remind friends and family of the person who died. Even when many years have passed and the wound seems to have healed, the recurrence of that day brings a sadness with it. Jay's sister died just two years ago and that day is more than just sad for him. It's still very painful.

"Like tonight, there's a dance here and I'll probably cry. You know, because it's the two-year anniversary," Jay says. "But I'll try my best not to!"

Other special days can be hard to deal with too. "At any kind of a celebration, it comes up," Adam states. His grandmother's annual birthday party is especially hard, not so much for him as for his parents.

"They always have a big party and all of that," he says. "She has thirteen grandchildren—and I'm used to hearing fourteen." The fact that the number is one less now strikes everyone. "For me, it was kind of OK," Adam says, "but then I looked at my mom and she was losing it."

Because of their strong associations with family, holidays can be difficult to handle for years. "Holidays were very rough 'cause it was extremely hard on my mother," Brenda recalls. "Christmas time, I can remember her crying a lot. That was one of the last times our whole family was together—on Christmas. It was hard to get used to Larry not being there."

If the death occurred over a holiday, the day has a double significance from then on. Not only is it a family event from which someone special is missing, but it's an anniversary as well. It's surprising how often this seems to happen.

Abby's brother died at the beginning of Passover. Now, five years later, Abby says, "There are certain times of the year when the Band-Aid peels off the wound, like Passover." The holiday is painful not only because it's the anniversary of Ben's death, but because it's such a family-oriented time. "There's always that extra chair, there's always that extra person missing," Abby says sadly.

Kristen's father died two days before Christmas. She was visiting relatives and he'd given them money to buy her a present. "So, I got this present and it said, 'From your dad,' and I started to cry," Kristen remembers. "'Cause how can I get a present from him when he's dead?"

The following Christmas, Kristen was miserable. Not only was it a holiday and the anniversary of her father's death, but a year had passed and the initial numbness had worn off, leaving Kristen very angry. "Last Christmas was really hard!" she states. "It wasn't so much Christmas, it was just that whole period. Because people who were my best friends, I didn't talk to. And when you don't talk to your best friends and you're upset because your father died, the whole world seems like it's collapsing."

Holidays and other special days may be sorrowful reminders, but they are also times when you are expected to celebrate and to be happy. For this reason, Jay was terrified that his sister would die on his birthday. He knew he'd never be able to enjoy the day again if she did.

"I mean, if she'd died on my birthday, I'd sort of never forgive myself or something," Jay struggles to explain. "Because every year, it's supposed to be your happy day! Then, all of a sudden, wham! This thing comes!"

Jay held his breath the whole day, waiting. Fortunately, his sister didn't die. "And after the day was gone," Jay remembers, "I thought, 'Thank you, God!'"

For adolescents whose mothers have died, Mother's Day can be especially difficult—not only because it's a painful reminder, but because everyone else is busy doing something with their moms. Terry and Stephanie had the misfortune to lose their mother on Mother's Day, making that day an anniversary as well. "We had cards and everything," Terry remembers. "She was in a coma but we read them to her and you could see her smiling."

This year on Mother's Day, Terry planted a bush at her mother's grave and spent the day with two close friends. "I just wanted to talk, you know," she says, "because it brought up a lot of memories."

Colin and his family bring flowers to the cemetery on the anniversary of his brother's death. Sharing his feelings with others at this time helps a lot too. "If you don't have anybody to talk to, it's a lonely feeling," he states. "But if people are around, it makes you feel better."

Because holidays and other celebrations are supposed to be fun, bereaved adolescents, like everyone else, want to enjoy them. But for people who have lost someone, these occasions can result in some very conflicting feelings. For Brenda's mother, holidays were painful reminders that only increased her sense of loss. Often her mother's grief kept Brenda from trying to get some pleasure from the day.

"I don't know if I resent my mother, but I'd get upset with her because she would sometimes ruin things on holidays," Brenda admits. "She'd cry because Larry wouldn't be there. And that would just get everyone in a bad mood." Brenda pauses for a moment. "But mostly, I felt sorry for her," she adds.

Jay handles these situations differently. He has a dance to go to and he's going to try to have fun. If he cries, well, then he cries. But just in case, he's asked a good friend to explain what's happening to others. "I told her, 'Just get ready for it tonight, because I might lose it.' And she said, 'No problem!'"

Part Five
Moving On

As A TURNING POINT between childhood and adulthood, adolescence is a time of contradictions, a mix-
ture of poignant loss and exhilarating opportunity.
As most teenagers prepare to leave the security of
their families for the exciting possibilities of the larger
world, they are buoyed by their own sense of invulner-
ability and by the knowledge that their parents are
there for them, ready to provide support if needed.
Bereaved adolescents, however, have been deprived
of this protective buffer. They've had to face the reality
that no one is invulnerable, that their families may
not always be able to provide safety and security.

How does the death of someone they loved affect
teenagers' transition into adulthood? How do they
incorporate this experience into their developing
sense of themselves? And, finally, how do they find
new ways of healing old wounds?

15 / New People/
New Places/New You

*I was kind of at that age where I was being shaped.
It's shaped me into an individual who feels that
people come first!*—ABBY

*I do find it really hard to get close to people
because I'm afraid they're going to go. I don't
think I'm stable enough to handle another
loss.*—MEGAN

ORDINARILY, adolescence is a series of progressive
separations. Teenagers increasingly break away from
their families, investing their emotional energy in
friends. In the course of moving from junior high
school to high school, they leave safe, familiar places
for new environments. Eventually, they leave in a
larger sense—going away to college or getting jobs
and their own apartments.

Under the best of circumstances, this process is
a difficult one. With each step, there is a potential
for loss. New friendships replace old ones and, even

if this is a conscious choice, something that once was important is now gone. Romances fall apart, often painfully for at least one person involved. New schools present challenges that may seem difficult to meet.

Surprisingly, many bereaved teenagers appear to handle the insecurity that results from these changes as well as any other adolescent. They make new friends, fall in love, and leave home with the same ease or difficulty as everyone else. However, even those bereaved adolescents who seem to cope well with separation and forming new relationships face some awkward situations in meeting new people and making new friends.

Julie's experience is typical of some of the problems involved. The year after her brother died, she moved to a new school. Not knowing what to say, Julie didn't mention his death to her new friends. "I made a bunch of friends and I never got around to telling them," she recalls. But when Julie gave a party, some of her friends noticed pictures of Denis. Julie was out of the room, so they asked her younger sister. "She tells everyone her whole life story," Julie says, "so she told them all."

Julie didn't mind that they knew. What was strange was that no one even mentioned it to her. She didn't find out until her mother told her what had happened. "No one said anything to me," Julie remembers. "I felt kind of awkward that they knew and they didn't say anything to me. It was weird."

Bereaved adolescents are not obligated to inform new friends but, particularly in the case of deceased parents, the facts eventually come out anyway. "They don't know why I never mention my mom," Terry says. "Because most people tend to talk about their mom rather than their dad." So, sooner or later, the topic comes up and she has to say something.

Even casual questions from new friends can have an unintended, loaded quality. "Before we adopted my little brother," Julie admits, "it was hard if someone asked, 'Do you have a brother?'"

Answering a question like this requires a delicate balance between being truthful and giving information that's appropriate in the context of a new relationship. "No, he died," can be a real conversation-stopper when two people are just getting to know each other.

Both Colin and Adam have found that new friends can have difficulty dealing with answers that are heavier than they expected to hear. "They get embarrassed, I found," Colin says. "They'll see a picture and say, 'Who's he?'" Colin's reply often makes them uncomfortable. "I don't get embarrassed," he adds. "It's more embarrassing for them." When friends from college see a picture of his brother and ask who he is, Adam tells them. But it's awkward. "I guess it's kind of a shock to them," he says.

Also, there's a hesitancy to say something about the death for fear it will alter the nature of the new friendship. "You're afraid that your relationship's going to change," Terry explains. "Because if you tell them, then they might be more careful about what they say to you and stuff."

Waiting too long, however, creates a different set of problems. "They get mad at you for *not* telling them," Stephanie complains. "They say, 'We've been friends for two whole months and you didn't tell me?' "

The ways they choose to cope with these situations are as different as the teenagers involved. Terry likes to get the whole thing over with as soon as possible in order to spare everyone future embarrassment. "I usually tell people right off the bat," she says.

Adam's approach is the opposite. He avoids the topic until he can no longer answer friends' questions honestly without mentioning his brother's death. "If someone at school says, 'Do you have any brothers?' I'll say, 'No.' 'Are you an only child?' I'll say, 'Yes.' But if they say, 'Do you like being an only child?' then I go into the story."

Awkward as these situations are, the problems they present are minor and temporary. Some bereaved teens have deeper difficulties in forming new relationships, however. Traumatized by the premature and permanent separation from someone they loved, they find it hard to get close to new people or to leave the safety of home. For them, the usual difficulties adolescents face in becoming independent adults have been heightened by the tremendous loss they have already experienced.

"A lot of the close relationships I had, I just pushed away," Megan says. "It was just too hard to be really close to someone, to be sharing things." Having felt abandoned by her mother, Megan didn't want to place herself in that position again. "I felt they were going to betray me," she admits. "I mean, I really felt betrayed by my mother."

Most threatening for Megan is the intimacy of romantic relationships. For a while, she went out with someone she liked, but she found it very rough going. "I was being very rude," Megan says, "and he kept saying, 'What's your problem?' And I thought, 'I've got to do something about this.' So I told him, 'You know, I'm having a very hard time trusting you. It's really hard!' I mean, he's a senior and I thought, 'You're going to be going away and I can't deal with another loss. I can't get close to you! I can't!'"

Since Brian's death, Pam hasn't really had another boyfriend. At first, she felt as though Brian would be mad if she went out. Then she realized he'd probably be mad if she didn't, if she just sat around waiting to die. So Pam's been dating, but without much success.

"It just doesn't work with guys," she says. "I mean, sometimes it seems to work and then suddenly it just doesn't. And it's not that I exactly relate it to Brian, but then I realize after it doesn't work, 'You know, that really does have to do with Brian.'"

Pam tends to compare everyone to Brian, of course, which she knows isn't good. But that's not the only problem. Like Megan, she gets frightened when the relationship begins to grow deeper.

"The longest I've stayed with somebody since Brian died was two months and one week," Pam recalls. "I noticed myself getting close. I noticed him starting to know me and to know my habits and I was noticing habits about him." At this point, Pam panicked. "Then I just got real scared! I said, 'No, I've got to get rid of this guy now before something bad happens and I get too close to him and I have to leave him later.'"

Having had a good relationship with Brian, Pam knows what she's missing by cutting herself off, so she's going to keep trying. It's hard, though.

Vicky's fears center more on leaving home than on forming new relationships. It took her family a long time to get close again after her mother's death and Vicky suffered a lot in the interim. Now the thought of leaving her family's support to go to college is very upsetting for her.

"It's going to be incredibly hard," Vicky says. "I think about it all the time. One of the major fears I have right now is leaving my family. We've become so close that it just seems so scary that they might leave or that I would leave."

Unfortunately, her one experience away from her family was a disaster. "I went to summer camp for two weeks when I was fourteen and I just cried every single night because I missed them," she remembers with a shudder. "I came home early. It tore my heart apart! I just couldn't stand to be away from them." As a result, Vicky is only considering colleges that are close to home.

Pam dreads leaving home too. "I don't even know if I want to go to school," she says hesitantly, although there's a college she's very interested in. What stops Pam is not so much the fear of leaving her family. For her, going away means finally leaving Brian. Pam still visits his grave to talk to him at least once a week and the comfort she gets from this is very important to her.

"Everyone seems to think it would be good for me to get away—and I agree," Pam acknowledges. "But I don't know if I can go away from the cemetery. I don't think I'm ready. But the only way I'll ever know is if I do," she adds.

For both Pam and Vicky, the death of someone they loved has affected their emotional readiness to leave home. But the death of a family member, especially if that person was a major source of financial support, can alter an adolescent's plans for the future in other ways as well.

Marie was planning to go to college, but her father's death made that impossible, at least for now. "I wanted to go to college right away, after high school," she says. "But my mother had trouble financially, so now I have to go to work.

"I spent the whole summer looking," she continues, "but I couldn't find a job, so I had to go to training school for three weeks." Marie has a job now, but she still hopes to be able to go to college—somewhere, sometime.

While having lost someone close can influence a teenager's future plans and relationships, the experience may have more subtle effects as well. Some of the teenagers interviewed for this book feel that the death of a person they loved has made a difference in who they are as people and in how they deal with life.

In some cases, the effect is fairly simple. As Stephanie puts it, "My dad couldn't really comfort me because he was in so much pain, so I had to become more independent."

Elaine feels that successfully handling the pain of Mandy's death has made her stronger. Now in her early twenties, she recently lost a close friend in an automobile accident. The pain was just as excruciating as before. "But I knew I'd get over it, that I'd be OK," she says. "Because I was able to cope with that first one. I told myself, 'You've been through this once, you can get through it again. You're going to hurt, but you're going to make it!'"

For Julie, experiencing the loss of her brother has made her more sensitive in general to other people's feelings. But this is particularly true in terms of grief. "Whenever someone I know has someone close to them die, I feel bad for them. More than I would if it hadn't happened to me, because I know what they're going through," she says.

Other teens have found the experience has altered their perception of themselves. "I don't know how to say it," Megan comments, "but I think it was an important experience. It taught me a lot about life. Not that I would have wanted it to happen," she hastens to add, "but I've learned a lot about myself through it and I've tried to improve myself."

Megan had a lot of painful feelings after her mother's death that were difficult for her to understand and accept. By acknowledging these emotions as part of the normal grieving process, she came to understand herself better too. "I accept myself more now," she concludes.

Like Megan, Abby and Pam also feel their experience helped them grow—sometimes faster than they wanted to. "For a while, I felt so old, like I was thirty or forty," says Pam. "Stuff that most teenagers do didn't seem like fun to me anymore."

Abby agrees. "When you're seventeen, you're kind of at that weird age when you're still learning and experiencing and growing," she comments. "You're not adult yet, but you're dealing with an adult situation, and that's hard. You lose some of your adolescence."

Part of this loss involved a change in Abby's priorities. "I noticed that I couldn't put up with things that were just so unimportant," she states. "Nothing else in this world matters but people! And I have a really hard time tolerating people who are phony, who are material."

The effect on Pam has been similar. "Sometimes I feel a lot more mature than some of my friends," she admits. "When I see a couple fight over something, I think, 'How could they be so stupid and so immature to fight over something like that when they don't even know what can happen?' So, it's changed me a lot."

Finally, after a death, surviving family members and friends may find their personalities shaped by their identification with the person who died. One way to keep the spirit of that person alive is to incorporate aspects of his or her personality into your own, thus letting the best parts of the person influence who you become. As long as this is done in moderation, it is a normal part of coping with loss.

"I'm really happy that there are parts of my personality that were influenced by him," Abby says of her brother Ben. "Sometimes I'll be sitting at the table talking to my mom and she'll just look at me and smile and say, 'That's such a Ben thing to do.' And it's not that I'm trying to be Ben," Abby explains. "It's just that part of him is in me."

Because the death has occurred at an important time in bereaved teenagers' own development, it is not surprising that this event may influence their values, sense of self, and view of the world. Painful and difficult as it may be, many of these young people are able to use their experience as an opportunity to learn more about themselves and to grow into more sensitive individuals.

16 / *Things That Happened Later That Made It Better*

Something did help me cope with it more. At graduation they had a memorial for her and I was chosen to write a poem.—ELAINE

My mom had a hard day. And she came home and said, "Carrie, if you're all right, give me a sign." All of a sudden a bluebird flew by! And it lifted her whole day.—JAY

Perhaps the hardest thing about the death of someone close is not losing the person but losing that person permanently. The chance to say what you wanted to say to them, to do what you wanted to do for them, is gone forever. Occasionally, though, another opportunity appears. You get a chance to do something, you learn something, or something special just seems to happen that changes how you feel about the death—that somehow makes things better.

Elaine felt robbed of her chance to say goodby to her best friend, Mandy. She wasn't told Mandy had cancer, much less that she was going to die, until after the last time she visited her in the hospital. Even then, she couldn't say anything to her friend because Mandy's parents didn't want their daughter to know she was dying. But two years later, at junior high school graduation, Elaine got a chance to say what she'd wanted to express earlier.

"At graduation, they wanted someone to speak about her death, so I wrote a poem and read it," Elaine says. "That was an emotional experience! It was my way of giving a gift to her, I guess, to her memory. And of saying goodby."

The last months of her brother's illness had been especially rough for Julie. Like all brothers and sisters, she and Denis had their share of squabbles. But Julie knew he was sick, and she tried hard to be considerate. "Since we were so close in age, we fought a lot, you know. And I held back a lot more," she remembers. "I went out of my way to be nice to him."

Denis was enough to try anyone's patience, though. He was in terrible pain and knew he was dying, and this made him mad at the world. "Well, the thing is that he got very grumpy. He was very angry and he'd yell at anything. It was very hard! He'd yell at the dog barking and whatever," Julie recalls.

Julie just struggled along anyhow, doing her best. It never occurred to her that Denis knew what she was going through. But it turned out that he did.

"My parents told me later that he used to tell them he felt bad that he would yell at me," Julie says. "He wouldn't tell *me* that," she adds. "He'd tell my parents. So I didn't know about this until later. But it was a good feeling when I heard about it."

Something else she hadn't known at the time was that Denis understood how hard it would be for her when he died. "He told my parents privately," Julie says softly, " 'Poor Julie,' because he knew he would leave me without a brother." Somehow, knowing he felt this way comforts her.

Bluebirds have a spiritual meaning for Jay's family. "Before my sister died," Jay says, "my mom said, 'If you die, you have to come back as bluebirds in my boxes.' Because my mom's always wanted bluebirds.

"So last year on May 6th [the anniversary of his sister's death], these bluebirds show up in our yard!" Jay exclaims. "And they nested there and they had babies. And my mom was going crazy!" From the look on Jay's face, his mother wasn't the only one who was glad to see the birds. To him, too, they're a message from his sister.

17 / Special Messages

THIS ENTIRE BOOK is, of course, a special message to bereaved teenagers and their families. But in talking about the feelings and problems they've faced, the young people who've shared their experiences with us here wanted to say certain things in particular to others who might be dealing with the death of someone they loved—things they've learned that have been especially important for them.

To Other Bereaved Adolescents

Talk to people, let it out. That will help a lot. Sometimes, when I feel alone, I write. Just put it in words. I think it helps.

Try to cope with the situation. Some people go and drink and things like that—that won't help anyway.—MARIE

Don't feel that you **have** *to cry. You shouldn't feel guilty if you don't cry.*

It will get better over time.—COLIN

It [sadness, pain] isn't going to come right away—it might, but it usually doesn't. You're not a bad person because you don't feel the pain right away.

Don't try to force yourself to talk about it right away. After a while, if you feel like it, you really should have at least one person you can talk to about it.

Remember, your feelings are not different from a lot of people who've gone through it.—JULIE

Don't try to do it alone. It's virtually impossible. And don't blame yourself.—PAM

You can't stop. Just because their time here ended, don't stop yours.—GARY

I don't mean to make it sound simple, but when somebody dies that you love, there's so much pain that you have to deal with. Why bother dealing with guilt?—ABBY

It's OK to be selfish—to feel sorry for yourself.

No matter how bad things get, they're always going to get better. Things were really horrible *for me, but things got better. You can get things back together again.*

*Just so you know—suicide isn't the
answer.*—STEPHANIE

*All I can say is that if you don't have anyone
to talk to, find somebody to talk to. Or at least
find something to talk to, like your pet. Because
that's the only way you can get it out. You can't
keep it inside because if you do, it's just going
to get worse and worse.*—JAY

Talk, talk, talk [to close friends].—TERRY

*It's going to hurt. And you are going to miss
the person.*

Don't feel badly about being alive.—ELAINE

The pain is not going to be like that forever.

*You shouldn't think you're crazy or that you're
an awful person because you don't want to think
about the person that died.*

*It's important to know that your feelings are
acceptable. Like I used to be really angry at my
mother [for dying].*

*You have to go on with your life. I felt guilty
about that.*—MEGAN

Just kind of go on. Don't let it hold you back. You know, don't sit there and say, 'Gee, he died, so it's over for me too.' Just take it in and go on with life.—ADAM

The biggest thing is to talk—just to get everything out that you feel.—BRENDA

To the Families and Friends of Bereaved Teenagers

If this happened to a friend of mine, I'd probably be quiet. I'd want to know what they have to say. And then I'd give them support in any way I could.—ERICA

Don't push them into talking about it right away.

Try to accept their feelings.—JULIE

Just be really supportive and understanding and accept what the person's going through. Just a genuine, "I'm going to be here for you. If you need me, here's a shoulder to cry on, here's my arm to hold you up."—MEGAN

Try to see if they want to talk about it. But don't force them.—COLIN

[To the families]. Be honest with the kid. Talk about dying and what you feel about it. Be sensitive to what they might be feeling, such as anger or even denial.—ELAINE

[To the families of kids who are having trouble]. Make them get help! Just pressure them, fight it as much as you can because a lot of bad things can turn out if they don't. Keep your eyes open to any little sign. And if you see that sign, don't avoid it because you're afraid to hurt them.—PAM

To Everyone

Talk! You must talk! Never feel, "So and so's dead already, what good is it going to do now?" What about all the other people that you love? Talk to them! Express what you feel for them. Say it before it's too late!—ABBY

Suggested Further Reading

Bernstein, Joanne. *Loss and How to Cope with It.*
Boston: Houghton Mifflin, 1976.

Griffin, Mary and Felsenthal, Carol. *Cry for Help.*
New York: Doubleday, 1983.

Guest, Judith. *Ordinary People.* New York: Viking-
Penguin, 1976.

Krementz, Jill. *How It Feels When a Parent Dies.*
New York: Alfred A. Knopf, 1983.

Raphael, Beverly. *The Anatomy of Bereavement.*
New York: Basic Books, 1983.

Index

ABOUT THE AUTHORS

KAREN GRAVELLE, Ph.D., MSW, previously worked as a psychotherapist in the field of drug addiction. She now writes for children and adolescents and is the co-author of Teenagers Face to Face with Cancer, *in addition to several books on science and animal behavior. Dr. Gravelle lives in New York City.*

CHARLES A. HASKINS, MSW, is an Episcopal priest as well as a certified social worker. Mr. Haskins is the director of a counseling center in New York City and works with both adults and adolescents. Additionally, he is Adjunct Professor of Pastoral Counseling at The General Seminary and an Associate Clergy at Christ and St. Stephen's Church in New York City.